Publications Handbook and Style Manual

1988

AMERICAN SOCIETY OF AGRONOMY
CROP SCIENCE SOCIETY OF AMERICA
SOIL SCIENCE SOCIETY OF AMERICA
677 South Segoe Road • Madison WI • 53711 • (608) 273-8080

ACKNOWLEDGMENT

Many persons contributed to the development and preparation of this *Publications Handbook and Style Manual*. Major impetus came from the Tri-Society Editorial Policy Coordinating Committee, consisting of D.R. Buxton, G.H. Heichel, E.L. Horner, C.W. Stuber, J.J. Mortvedt, and D.E. Kissel. Assisting them was a headquarters office committee consisting of D.M. Kral, R.C. Dinauer, W.R. Luellen, S.H. Mickelson, and Susan Ernst. Other society officers and members as well as headquarters staff employees contributed assistance and suggestions. William R. Luellen served as managing editor, Barbara S. Littlewood prepared the index, and Patricia Jeffson designed the cover.

American Society of Agronomy, Inc.
Crop Science Society of America, Inc.
Soil Science Society of America, Inc.
677 South Segoe Road, Madison, Wisconsin 53711 USA

Library of Congress Cataloging in Publication Data

Publications handbook and style manual.

Bibliography: p.
Includes index.
1. Agriculture—Authorship—Handbooks, manuals, etc. 2. Authorship—Style manuals. I. American Society of Agronomy. II. Crop Science Society of America. III. Soil Science Society of America.
S494.5.A96P83   1988   808'.06663   88-16703
ISBN 0-89118-096-6

Printed in the United States of America

Contents

Chapter 1. Introduction

Dissemination of information is one of the primary functions of the American Society of Agronomy, Crop Science Society of America, and Soil Science Society of America.

Publications from the three societies cover the following areas: (i) original research reports in agronomy, crop science, soil science, environmental quality, production agriculture, and agronomic education; (ii) reviews of research in these fields; (iii) symposia proceedings; (iv) monographs and textbooks; (v) abstracts of papers presented at the annual meetings; (vi) official business of the societies; (vii) news, events, and announcements; and (viii) semitechnical articles.

The general editorial policies and practices of the societies are determined by the respective boards of directors, whose members are elected. Responsibility for maintaining editorial standards and advising on publication policy is delegated to editors-in-chief, editorial boards, and editors. A separate committee coordinates editorial policies and procedures among the societies. The societies' headquarters office staff manages the publications.

This *Publications Handbook and Style Manual* serves as a guide for authors in preparing manuscripts and other material submitted for publication by the societies. It replaces an earlier manual published in 1984, and should be used as a primary source for writing, style, editing, and procedures for publications of the associated societies. An *Editors' Handbook*, also published by the three societies, provides specific information for those with editorial responsibilities on journals, books, or monographs, and is available to them at no charge. Other books, e.g., the *CBE Style Manual* (Counc. of Biol. Ed., 1983) and *The Chicago Manual of Style* (Univ. of Chicago Press, 1982), may be used as supplements and expansions on these subjects.

1

Chapter 2. Journal Management and Procedures

Much of the administration and all the printing, production, and distribution of the publications are coordinated by the headquarters office staff. This section gives an overview of the present responsibilities and practices in the review, handling, and production of publications of ASA, CSSA, and SSSA. Additional details and supplementary information are available from the headquarters office.

ELIGIBILITY OF AUTHORS

At least one author of each unsolicited manuscript reviewed and published by *Agronomy Journal, Crop Science*, or *SSSA Journal* must be an active, emeritus, sustaining member representative, graduate student, or dues-paying undergraduate student member of one or more of the three societies. Exceptions to this rule may be granted by the president of the sponsoring society. Authors of manuscripts published by the *Journal of Environmental Quality, Journal of Production Agriculture*, or *Journal of Agronomic Education* do not need to be members of any of the three societies.

MANUSCRIPT HANDLING

The journals generally handle manuscripts by similar procedures. Four copies of manuscripts, tables, and figures are required by all journals. Manuscripts for *Crop Science* and *Journal of Agronomic Education* should be sent to the managing editor at the headquarters office. Contributions to the *SSSA Journal* should be sent to the editor-in-chief, and those to *Agronomy Journal, Journal of Production Agriculture*, and the *Journal of Environmental Quality* should be sent to the respective editor at the addresses indicated in the mastheads of these journals.

3

Receipt of manuscripts is acknowledged and authors are informed as review, approval or release, and publication occur. Correspondence about revisions to the manuscript occurs between associate or consulting editors, technical editor or editors, and authors. A manuscript, when approved by the editor, is prepared for printing by the headquarters office.

Papers may be transferred from one society journal to another with permission of the editors and authors involved.

PUBLICATION CHARGES

Publication charges are assessed for regular volunteer papers and notes accepted by scientific journals of the societies. Current charges are published in the journals' masthead. No publication charges are assessed for invited papers or for letters to the editor. Journal author alterations at the proof stage are charged separately, and an extra charge is assessed if costs exceed the average for reproduction of line drawings or photographs.

PRIOR PUBLICATION

Manuscripts published in the scientific journals must be original reports. They may not have been published previously or simultaneously submitted to another scientific or technical journal. Whether publication in nontechnical outlets constitutes prior publication is decided on a case-by-case basis. In general, publication in nontechnical media will be considered prior publication only when all of the data and conclusions are included in the nontechnical media.

NOTES

Notes are a separate category of papers, not merely papers that are too insubstantial to be considered as regular research papers. Notes are used to describe research techniques, apparatus, and observations of unique (usually unrepeatable, such as hail or frost damage) phenomena. Notes are usually shorter than research papers, normally occupying less than two printed pages in the journal.

An article submitted as a note will receive a registration number similar to that given a research paper, except that the number is followed by a capital "N." The review procedure for notes is identical to that for research papers.

Occasionally an editor may believe a paper submitted as a research paper will better fit the criteria established for notes. If the author agrees, the manuscript can be transferred to that section of the journal.

LETTERS TO THE EDITOR

All the societies' journals publish letters to the editor. Letters may contain comments on articles appearing in the journals or general discussions about agronomic research, and are limited to one printed page. Letters must be approved by the editor of the journal and may receive a peer review. If a letter discusses a published paper, the author of that paper may submit a response to the comments. This response is generally published along with the letter.

EDITORS-IN-CHIEF

Each society has an editor-in-chief, nominated by the president and confirmed by the board of directors. Each editor-in-chief serves a 3-year term and may be reappointed for one additional term. These persons have overall responsibility for all publications of the respective societies and serve on the intersociety editorial policy coordination committee, which is chaired by the ASA Editor-in-Chief.

Each editor-in-chief makes recommendations to that society's president about appointment and reappointment of editors of journals and other publications, and serves as a member of all editorial boards and publication committees of that society. These persons may be called on to handle special problems through an appeals process and to perform other editorial duties requested by the board of directors.

OTHER EDITORS

Technical, associate, and consulting editors for each scientific journal are appointed by the president of the respective society for 3-year terms and may be reappointed once.

AGRONOMY JOURNAL

Agronomy Journal, a publication of the American Society of Agronomy, is published six times a year. The editorial board consists of the editor-in-chief of ASA; an editor; a managing editor; technical editors in crops, soils, agroclimatology, and agronomic modeling; a number of associate editors; the executive vice president; and the vice president—management and operations.

Articles relating to original research in soil-plant relationships; crop science; soil science; biometry; crop, soil, pasture, and range management; crop, forage, and pasture production and utilization; turfgrass; agroclimatology and agronomic modeling; and computer software are published in *Agronomy Journal* subsequent to review and approval by the editorial board. Articles should make a significant contribution to the advancement of knowledge or toward a better understanding of existing agronomic concepts. The study reported must be of potential interest to a significant number of scientists and, if specific to a local situation, must be relevant to a wide body of knowledge in agronomy. Additional details on requirements for articles are published in *Agronomy Journal* each year.

Review papers that are either volunteered or invited by the editorial board may be printed in the journal. Invitational papers from nonmembers may be published on approval by the president if found acceptable by the editorial board.

Responsibilities

Editor

The editor, chair of the editorial board, is responsible for overall quality of the content of the journal, and implements policy decisions approved by the board of directors. The editor and editorial board oversee procedures for manuscript submission, acceptance, release, publication, and the criteria for review and referee of papers. The editor delegates editorial functions to other members of the editorial board and takes an active part in defining the journal's aims, policies, and editorial coverage. The editor receives manuscripts, assigns the papers to technical editors, keeps records of the status of manuscripts in review, and handles the appeal procedure for manuscripts that are rejected. The editor may write editorials or solicit manuscripts on special topics.

Technical Editor

Technical editors are responsible for the technical and intellectual content of the journal in their assigned areas. They direct the work of assigned associate editors in reviewing and evaluating manuscripts submitted to the journal. They may delegate to associate editors the responsibility of corresponding and working with authors when revisions of manuscripts are needed. Technical editors notify authors when manuscripts are unworthy for publication and inform the managing editor and editor of this action, but it is the managing editor who notifies authors of acceptance of their manuscripts for publication.

Associate Editor

Associate editors are responsible for obtaining a minimum of two reviews and for evaluating, in a timely manner, the technical and intellectual content and suitability of manuscripts assigned to them. Associate editors make a recommendation to the technical editor about a course of action regarding the disposition of assigned manuscripts but do not approve or reject manuscripts.

Managing Editor

The managing editor for *Agronomy Journal* is assigned by the vice president—management and operations. The managing editor notifies authors of the acceptance of their manuscript for publication and its probable publication date, and supervises the steps in copyediting papers for publication, typesetting, sending galley proofs to authors, preparing papers for printing, and producing reprints.

Manuscript Handling

General Procedures

Manuscripts should be submitted in quadruplicate to the editor who verifies that at least one of the authors is eligible to publish, assigns a registration number, notifies the corresponding author of receipt of the manuscript, and sends the author a "Permission to Print and Reprint" form (see Chapter 8). The registration number must be used in all correspondence regarding the manuscript. The editor assigns the manuscript to a technical editor on the basis of the subject matter. The technical editor, in turn, assigns properly prepared manuscripts to an associate editor. The associate editor obtains a minimum of two reviews.

If the reviewers recommend publication without change and the associate editor agrees, the manuscript and reviewer reports are sent to the technical editor for concurrence.

If the reviewers and the associate editor find that the manuscript could be published after some revision, the manuscript is returned to the author to obtain a satisfactory revision.

If the reviewers and associate editor recommend that a manuscript be rejected, the manuscript and reviewers' comments are sent to the technical editor. If the technical editor concurs that the manuscript should be rejected, the technical editor releases the manuscript to the author.

If a manuscript returned to an author for revision is not returned within 26 weeks it will be released by the technical editor. Once released, manuscripts must be resubmitted to the editor to receive additional consideration by the journal.

Preparation of Papers for Publication

Approved manuscripts are prepared for printing in order of their received dates. Manuscripts are read and edited by the managing editor or an assistant editor. The author may be contacted concerning editorial problems.

Galley proofs are sent to the authors along with the manuscript, figure proofs, table proofs, and a reprint order form showing the page and publication charges.

A total of about 15 days is allowed for proofing (inclusive of mail transit time to and from the author). Air mail is used to send proofs to foreign countries and should be used for their return.

The production and shipping of reprints is managed by the headquarters office. About 6 weeks are required from delivery of the journal to shipment of reprints.

JOURNAL OF AGRONOMIC EDUCATION

The *Journal of Agronomic Education* (JAE) is published twice each year by the ASA. The journal accepts reports of original studies pertaining to concepts of resident, extension, and industrial education in crop and soil sciences. Authors of manuscripts submitted to JAE are not required to be members of one of the three societies. Reviews or digests of a comprehensive and well-defined scope are acceptable. The journal also prints notes, articles describing slide sets, computer software, newsfeatures, profiles, ideas, book reviews, editorials, and letters to the editor. Articles may confirm and strengthen the findings of others, revise established ideas or practices, or challenge accepted theory, providing the evidence presented is significant and convincing. Manuscripts based mainly on personal philosophy or opinion are acceptable if they conform to the above criteria.

The editorial board consists of the editor-in-chief of ASA, an editor, a number of associate editors, a managing editor, the executive vice president, and the vice president—management and operations.

Manuscripts intended for JAE must be prepared according to the instructions in this manual and sent in quadruplicate to the managing editor at headquarters office. The managing editor notifies the corresponding author of receipt of the manuscript and assigns it a registration number that must be used in all correspondence regarding the manuscript. The managing editor sends the manuscript to an associate editor who obtains a minimum of two reviews. The duties of the editorial board and the remaining steps toward publication are similar to those for *Agronomy Journal*. Appeals of decisions are handled by the editor-in-chief of ASA.

JOURNAL OF ENVIRONMENTAL QUALITY

The *Journal of Environmental Quality* (JEQ) is published quarterly by the ASA, CSSA, and SSSA. The JEQ editorial board consists of the editor-in-chief of ASA, an editor, associate and consulting editors, a managing editor, the executive vice president, and the vice president—management and operations.

Consulting editors are not required to be members of the three societies. Their responsibilities and those of the associate editors are similar to those listed for associate editors of *Agronomy Journal*.

Authors of manuscripts submitted to JEQ are not required to be members of one of the three societies. Contributions reporting original research or brief reviews and analyses dealing with some aspect of environmental quality in natural and agricultural ecosystems are accepted from all disciplines for consideration by the editorial board. Manuscripts may be volunteered, invited, or coordinated as a symposium. Acceptance of a group of symposium manuscripts for collective publication is limited to one such group per issue. Book reviews may be invited by the editor.

Papers in JEQ cover various aspects of anthropogenic impacts on the environment, with particular focus on terrestrial and aquatic systems. Emphasis is given to the understanding of underlying processes rather than to monitoring, and papers should be broad in scope. Topics receiving attention in the Journal include: reutilization of agricultural, municipal and industrial wastes; transport, transformations, fate, and ecological impact of nutrients, pesticides, and toxic organics; impacts of acid precipitation on plants, soils, and aquatic biota; and reclamation and management of drastically disturbed lands. Short papers concerning experimental observations or development of methods will be treated as technical reports.

Contributions to JEQ should be submitted in quadruplicate to the editor at the address listed in the masthead of each issue. All manuscripts deemed suitable for review are given a registration number that specifies whether the manuscript is a technical report or review and analyses paper.

The editor notifies the corresponding author of receipt of the paper and assigns it a registration number that must be used in all correspondence regarding the manuscript. The editor assigns each manuscript to an associate or consulting editor according to field of specialization.

The remaining procedures are essentially the same as described for *Agronomy Journal*. Appeals of decisions by the editorial board are handled by the ASA Editor-in-Chief.

JOURNAL OF PRODUCTION AGRICULTURE

The *Journal of Production Agriculture* (JPA) is published quarterly by the ASA, CSSA, and SSSA. The American Agricultural Economics Association, American Forage and Grassland Council, American Society of Animal Science, the Weed Science Society of America, and the Society for Range Management are cooperators in the publication. The editorial board consists of the editor-in-chief of ASA, an editor, associate and consulting editors, a managing editor, the executive vice president, and the vice president—management and operations.

Authors of manuscripts submitted to JPA are not required to be members of one of the three societies. Contributions may be submitted in the form of technical articles, review articles, notes, articles on contemporary issues, letters to the editor, editorials, or book reviews. Manuscripts may be volunteered or invited.

Articles published in this journal transfer production-oriented information to a wide range of professional agriculturalists. Emphasis will be placed on information related to agronomy in concert with other disciplines such as animal science, weed science, agricultural economics, entomology, plant pathology, horticulture, and forestry. All manuscripts must use the Customary (inch-pound) system of measurement unless a commonly accepted unit does not exist for the item being measured. Standard SI units may be included parenthetically in the text or as footnotes in tables and figures. More details on manuscript preparation are published in the journal each year.

Authors should submit four legible copies of their manuscript to the editor at the address listed in the masthead of each issue. The editor notifies the corresponding author of receipt of the paper and assigns a registration number, which should be used in all correspondence regarding the manuscript. The editor sends the manuscript to an associate or consulting editor who reviews it and obtains at least one additional review. All manuscripts, whether volunteered or invited, are subject to review.

The remaining procedures are basically the same as described for *Agronomy Journal*. The ASA Editor-in-Chief handles the appeal procedure for released manuscripts.

CROP SCIENCE

Crop Science, published bimonthly, is the official publication of the Crop Science Society of America. The publication is prepared by an editorial board consisting of an editor and editor-in-chief, technical editors, associate editors, a managing editor, the executive vice president, and the vice president—management and operations. Technical editors handle manuscripts in crop genetics, breeding, cytology, and statistics; crop physiology and metabolism; and ecology, production, seed and turf science, and utilization.

Crop Science publishes original research in crop genetics, breeding, cell biology, molecular genetics, cytology, physiology, management, ecology, quality, utilization, and pest management. Critical reviews may also be published. Papers in all the above categories should be submitted, in quadruplicate, to the managing editor who gives each paper a registration number that should be used in all correspondence concerning the paper. The managing editor assigns the paper to a technical editor who supervises the review process. Cultivar, germplasm, parental line, and genetic stock registrations are published after review by a crop registration committee. Authors should submit registrations to the crop registration subcommittee member for the specific crop or to the crop registration committee chair. Their names and addresses are listed in the masthead of each issue.

All papers, whether invited or volunteered, are subject to review. Additional details on requirements for articles are published in *Crop Science* each year. Appeals of decisions by the editorial board are handled by the editor. The rest of the procedures and responsibilities of editorial board members are similar to those of *Agronomy Journal*, except that the time allowed by *Crop Science* for author revisions is 13 weeks.

SOIL SCIENCE SOCIETY OF AMERICA JOURNAL

The *Soil Science Society of America Journal* (*SSSA Journal*), published bimonthly, is the official publication of the Soil Science Society of America. The editorial board consists of an editor-in-chief, technical editors, associate editors (including at least one representative for each division of SSSA), a managing editor, the executive vice president, and the vice president—management and operations.

The *SSSA Journal* publishes papers on original research, reviews of research, and comments and letters to the editor. Papers of appropriate subject matter usually less than two printed pages may be submitted as notes. Invitational papers may be published in the journal if accepted by the editorial board.

Contributions to the *SSSA Journal* should be submitted in quadruplicate to the editor-in-chief, whose name and address are given in the masthead of each issue. For further details, see SSSA Publication Policy and the Suggestions to Contributors that are published in the January–February issue of each volume. The editor-in-chief notifies the corresponding author of receipt of the manuscript and assigns it a registration number that must be used in all correspondence regarding the manuscript. The editor-in-chief assigns each manuscript to the technical editor supervising the division in which the paper will be reviewed. The technical editor will assign the manuscript to an associate editor according to field of specialization. The remaining steps are essentially the same as those described for *Agronomy Journal*, except that associate editors have the authority to approve manuscripts for publication. Manuscripts judged to be unsuitable for publication are referred back to the technical editor who makes the final decision to release these manuscripts. Authors of such manuscripts should contact the editor-in-chief if they wish to appeal the decision.

Chapter 3. Procedures for Monographs, Books, and Other Publications

In addition to their scientific journals, the three societies publish monographs, books, special publications, *Agronomy Abstracts*, *Agronomy News*, an annual meeting program, slide sets, glossaries, and miscellaneous papers and booklets.

Honorariums are not paid, but as a token of appreciation for their efforts, each author and editor of a monograph, book, or special publication receives a free copy of the published version. In addition, 200 reprints of each chapter are given to (or divided among) the author(s) of that chapter.

MONOGRAPHS

A monograph is a detailed, scholarly treatise written by experts on a single topic or commodity. Monographs are published on an irregular schedule, only after a committee of specialists determines a need for monographic treatment of a topic.

When a topic for a new monograph or revision of an existing monograph is proposed, the monographs committee reviews the topic. If the committee recommends that the subject merits further study, it may submit its recommendation to the appropriate executive committee or may suggest the names of scientists for appointment to an ad hoc "monograph feasibility committee." The feasibility committee reports to the monographs committee on (i) need for the proposed monograph; (ii) quantity and quality of research information available on the monograph topic; (iii) existence of, or plans for, books on the same topic; and (iv) potential sales volume.

Based on the feasibility committee report, the monographs committee may recommend through the ASA President that a monograph on the topic be prepared. The societies' executive committee(s) or board(s) makes the final decision on publication of the monograph.

The monographs committee nominates persons for membership on specific monograph editorial committees to the appropriate society president who appoints an editor and editorial committee to develop the monograph. The monographs committee reviews outlines from the editor of the monograph to ensure that the general content and distribution of authorship of the proposed monograph is consistent with the goals of the sponsoring society(ies). The monograph's editor(s) then negotiates a final outline with individual authors.

Duties of the Editor and Editorial Committee

The editor and editorial committee are responsible for the preparation, review, and editing of the monograph. This includes determining the scope of the monograph, organizing subject matter, selecting qualified authors, providing uniformity in style, and technical editing of manuscripts.

The editor and members of the editorial committee may serve as authors, and an author may prepare more than one chapter. The editor of the monograph advises authors on the scope and intended audience for the monograph. Authors do not need to be members of any of the societies. Authors should be apprised of their responsibilities relating to completion of manuscripts and give written consent to prepare the manuscript within a prescribed time. Details are covered in the *Editors' Handbook* (1988).

Duties and Responsibilities of Chapter Authors

Authors are responsible for: preparing and submitting detailed chapter outlines; first drafts of the manuscript, typed double-spaced on line-numbered paper (available at no charge from headquarters); a final draft of the manuscript; correcting proofs; a subject index, if requested by the editor; and written permission from the owners to use any copyrighted material (see Chapter 8).

Manuscripts for monograph chapters should be submitted according to deadlines agreed on with the editor. The editor or editorial committee may replace authors who do not meet deadlines or who provide unsatisfactory manuscripts.

Authors should prepare complete, up-to-date, definitive chapters covering the assigned subject matter. They are responsible for the interpretation they place on the published literature, and should make critical analyses of reported research results. Authors should obtain in-house institutional or agency reviews of their chapters, and institutional clearance before submitting manuscripts to the editor. The editor should be informed of who reviewed the manuscripts because the monograph editorial committee will ask other specialists for independent peer reviews of the chapters.

Authors are responsible for the costs involved in preparation of their manuscripts, including illustrations. They must agree that material in the manuscript will be published first by the associated societies and that the societies, as publishers, will control its subsequent distribution via transfer of copyright (see Chapter 8).

Authors should use this manual as the official guide for preparing their manuscripts. When the requirements differ for the various societies, those given for ASA publications should be followed. The editor should inform authors of any special procedures to ensure uniformity in style of writing for the text, units of measurements, scientific names, literature references, illustrations, etc.

Duties of Headquarters Staff

When all manuscripts have been received by headquarters, a managing editor is assigned. The managing editor corresponds directly with the editor and corresponding authors about questions requiring their attention. Proofs of each chapter are sent to authors for proofreading. Corrected proofs are sent to the authors or the monograph editor for completion of the index. The managing editor asks the editor to prepare a preface, and asks the presidents of the societies sponsoring the monograph to prepare a foreword.

The headquarters office secures a copyright for the book. All promotion, sales, and distribution are the responsibility of the staff at headquarters office.

SSSA BOOK SERIES

The Soil Science Society of America sponsors a book series. The procedures for choosing the subject matter, assigning editor(s) and editorial committee, and preparation and editing of manuscripts are similar to those used in the monographs series.

BOOKS

Subject matter of books is usually not covered in as much depth as in monographs, and covers a broader aspect of a particular subject than a special publication.

Books can be a compilation of papers presented at special society(ies)-sponsored symposia or conferences, a compilation of papers written by a number of authors on a particular subject but not presented at a symposium, or a manuscript written by a single author. The societies may consider for publication unsolicited manuscripts that further the educational goals of the societies.

Proposals for books should be submitted to the executive vice president or the vice president—management and operations. The executive committees make a decision on publication after consultation with the respective editors-in-chief.

If the papers for the book are presented at a special symposium, a symposium planning committee is appointed by the societies' presidents. The committee develops sessions, outlines topics, and selects participants who become authors of the papers. The executive committee, in consultation with the respective editor-in-chief, appoints an editorial committee, which reviews manuscripts. Approval of a publication does not constitute approval of the manuscript(s), which must be reviewed and approved by the editor of the publication. See also the monographs section of this book and the *Editors' Manual* (1988) for duties of the editor, editorial committee, authors, and headquarters staff.

SPECIAL PUBLICATIONS

Paperbound special publications usually result from timely topics presented from symposia at the annual meetings of the societies. Each society has its own special publication series. The ASA, CSSA, and SSSA can jointly publish any of the series.·

Guidelines

Organizing Committee

Members who initiate a special publication submit a proposal for a special publication, on a form available from headquarters office, to the executive vice president or the vice president—management and operations. A proposal to publish the proceedings of a symposium must be submitted at least 26 weeks before the symposium. Proposals are submitted to the society program officer, who, in turn, submits them to the executive vice president or the vice president—management and operations.

The executive committees of the three societies review special publication proposals, and after consultation with the editors-in-chief of the societies, approve or disapprove publishing the special publication. For a special publication sponsored jointly by all three societies, ASA assumes leadership. If the publication is jointly sponsored by ASA and CSSA, CSSA assumes leadership. If ASA and SSSA are joint sponsors, SSSA assumes leadership.

Editorial Committee

The executive committee may appoint an editorial committee for a special publication from persons recommended in the proposal. The editor should keep the editor(s)-in-chief of the society(ies) apprised of the publication's progress. The editor-in-chief of the leadership society serves as an ex-officio member of the editorial committee.

Handling of Manuscripts

Papers for a special publication, whether invited or volunteered, must be submitted to the organizer of the symposium or the editor of the special publication at least 4 weeks before the symposium. The authors of such papers must submit a Transfer of Copyright form to the society (see Chapter 8).

Manuscripts submitted to the chair of the editorial committee are assigned to members of the committee for review as outlined below. Manuscripts should meet society publication standards. The chair makes the final decision on the acceptability of manuscripts.

Timeliness of publication of symposia papers is crucial to fulfilling the purposes justifying publication, commitments to authors, and successful sales. Hence, editorial work must be completed promptly and manuscripts sent to the managing editor, normally within 8 weeks after the date of the symposium. Delays greatly exceeding this will cause the society executive committee to reevaluate its commitment to publish.

Review of Manuscripts

Manuscripts that are primarily presentations of original data are reviewed to determine that (i) experimental methods and procedures are adequately described, (ii) interpretations and conclusions are valid and consistent with the data presented, and (iii) the paper presents significant new information or a significant new interpretation of preexisting data.

Contents of manuscripts that are primarily reviews and interpretations of published data are reviewed to determine that (i) all aspects of the topic have been adequately covered, (ii) data presented are representative of the information published, and (iii) the interpretations and conclusions made are consistent with the data and results presented. Authors of such papers must obtain permission to use existing material from the author(s) and publisher(s) of that material.

Reviewers of manuscripts being considered for publication have 4 weeks to review the manuscripts. The authors have 4 weeks to make the revisions and return the manuscripts to the editor of the special publication.

AGRONOMY NEWS

Agronomy News is the official monthly newsletter of the three societies. Members and nonmembers alike may submit items for publication under the following categories:

1. People (names and events in the news)
2. Miscellaneous
3. Calendar
4. Meetings
5. Publications
6. Software abstracts
7. Retirements
8. Deaths
9. Personnel (positions and assistantships wanted and available)
10. Lists of theses and dissertations (annually)

The newsletter is published monthly. The publication's editor should be contacted for specific questions. Deadlines are published in the newsletter. Articles may be submitted by individuals or organizations. Publication charges are not assessed for publishing articles.

Photographs are an excellent addition for many articles. Although color photos are occasionally acceptable, black-and-white photos are preferred. Gray photos reproduce poorly. The background in photos should be simple. Refer to Chapter 6 in this manual for further information and to *The Associated Press Stylebook and Libel Manual* (French et al., 1980) or a recent issue of *Agronomy News* for help in preparing material for the newsletter.

Chapter 4. Preparing the Manuscript

Manuscripts submitted to society journals, monographs, books, and special publications are critically reviewed before they are published. The purpose of the review is to assure readers that the papers have been found acceptable by competent, independent professionals. The process often results in desirable changes in the manuscripts, but it is not a substitute for the author's maximum efforts to present the best possible report of findings.

Every paper should have a thorough review by competent colleagues of the author before it is submitted for publication.

Authors should study this section, applicable writing sections in the *CBE Style Manual*, and recent publications of the three societies before preparing manuscripts. Any submitted paper not conforming to acceptable standards will be returned to authors for reworking before review.

The formats used in society journals, books, special publications, and other media differ. This chapter covers formats that can be readily identified and described, but the discussion applies to other formats to varying degrees. The following chapters (Chapters 5 and 6) should also be consulted for details of style because the principles of precision, logic, and clarity in presentation pertain to all manuscripts submitted to the society.

MANUSCRIPT FORMAT FOR JOURNAL ARTICLES

Manuscripts prepared for society journals should usually be arranged in the following order:

1. Title and author(s).
2. Author/paper documentation at bottom of the same page.
3. Abstract.
4. Introduction (includes literature review). This section is not labeled with a section heading. Such headings are used on the abstract and the following four sections, however.
5. Materials and methods.
6. Results. This section is sometimes combined with the discussion.
7. Discussion. This section may be combined with a conclusions section. A separate summary section should not be used because it will

duplicate information in the abstract, but a summary statement can be given as a closing paragraph.

8. References.
9. Tables and figures.

In some papers other headings or subheadings may be used, e.g., theory, description of study area, soil profile description. Limited use of subheadings is encouraged to highlight significantly different aspects of the methods, results, or discussion sections. The review articles and notes are usually less formal than full-length articles. Letters to the editor are not divided into sections.

Title and Author(s)

The title should represent the article's content and facilitate retrieval in indexes developed by secondary literature services.

A good title (i) briefly identifies the subject, (ii) indicates the purpose of the study, and (iii) gives important, high-impact words early. A person usually decides to read an article based on the title's content.

Besides being descriptive, titles should be short. The societies recommend that titles not exceed 12 words, except in unusual circumstances. A title containing fewer than five words probably should be expanded.

The meaning and order of words in a title are also important. Do not start the title with low-impact words such as "Effect of" or "Influence of." Instead, concentrate on the subject and findings of the research. The title must be useful in itself as a label. The terms in the title should be limited to those words that give significant information about the article's content.

Many readers peruse the titles in a table of contents to decide whether or not to turn to a given abstract. The title must interest these readers. Overly specific, narrow titles with words understandable only to specialists will be passed over. Further, literature searchers will ignore titles that are incomprehensible to all but a few individuals.

Titles should never contain abbreviations, chemical formulas, or proprietary names; and authors should avoid using unusual or outdated terminology.

For economy of space, common names of chemicals and crops should be used in titles. If a crop or microorganism has no common name, then the scientific name (genus and species) is used.

Series titles are used infrequently in society journals. An author contemplating whether or not to prepare a series of articles on the same subject should refer to the current editorial policy of the journal. Articles in a series are not discouraged on that basis alone, but the editors need to be assured that all papers in the series are available for review and that the reader can obtain previously and later published material in that series. The series publication of papers also presents scheduling problems in production of the journal.

In the by-line, authors' names or initials are published as they appear on the manuscript. An asterisk (*) follows the name of the corresponding author and the person from whom reprints should be requested.

Author/Paper Documentation

A new single-paragraph format for author and paper documentation was initiated with this style manual edition. This new item replaces footnotes 1 and 2. The paragraph appears in the same place in the printed journal as did the earlier two footnotes. In the manuscript the paragraph is typed at the bottom of the page containing the title and author names. The abstract begins at the top of the next manuscript page.

The new paragraph lists author(s) and complete address(es) first, sponsoring organization(s) with incomplete address(es) second, date received (added later at headquarters) third, and "*Corresponding author" last. Professional titles are not listed. Other information, such as grant funding, may be included before the date of receipt in this paragraph or in the acknowledgment at the end of the paper. If there is only one author or if all authors have the same address, the name(s) is (are) not repeated in the author/paper documentation. Below is an example of a by-line and the corresponding author/paper documentation:

A. Bertram Smith, Charles D. Jones,* and E. F. Brown

A.B. Smith and E.F. Brown, Dep. of Agronomy, 1102 S. Goodwin Ave., Univ. of Illinois, Urbana, IL 61801; and C.D. Jones, Dep. of Agronomy, Purdue Univ., West Lafayette, IN 47907. Joint contribution of the Illinois and Indiana Agric. Exp. Stn. Purdue Journal no. 1234. Received 11 Jan. 1988. *Corresponding author.

Abstract

A person reading the abstract should be able to tell quickly the value of the report and whether to read further. In many cases, more people will read the abstract than will read the entire report. Thus, the abstract has the dual function of supplying information to those who will read the entire report and to those who will read nothing further of the paper.

The abstract should be a suitable literary adjunct to the printed paper. It should be written after the paper is completed and should be consistent with statements in the paper. To some extent the abstract will repeat wording in the paper, but because it is sometimes read immediately before the introduction or other main sections, it should not be a tedious recapitulation.

On the other hand, the abstract must be completely self-explanatory and intelligible in itself. It should include the following:

1. Reason for doing work, including rationale or justification for the research.
2. Objectives and topics covered.
3. Brief description of methods used. If the paper deals mainly with methods, give the basic principles, range, and degree of accuracy for new methods.

4. Results.

5. Conclusions.

The abstract also should call attention to new items, observations, and numerical data. Abstracts should be informative. Expressions such as "is discussed" and "is described" should rarely be included. Specific rather than general statements must be used, especially in the methods and results sections of the abstract. For example, do not say "two rates of P" but say "rates of 40 and 80 kg of P ha^{-1}."

The abstract should not exceed 250 words for full-length papers and 100 words for notes, and is not divided into paragraphs. It should not include bibliographic, figure, or table references. Equations, formulas, obscure abbreviations, and acronyms also are inappropriate. The scientific names of plants, insects, etc., full chemical names, and identification of soil if the soil type is a factor in interpreting the results, must be included in the abstract when the common names are first mentioned.

With permission of the author, a published abstract is reproduced here broken apart with its sections labeled. Study it to see both overall construction of the abstract and the contents of each of its parts. [From *Agron. J.* 78:720–726 (1986), updated to conform to new style guidelines.]

Dryland Grain Sorghum Water Use, Light Interception, and Growth Responses to Planting Geometry

J. L. Steiner*

ABSTRACT

Rationale   Crop yields are primarily water-limited under dryland production systems in semiarid regions.

Objectives   This study was conducted to determine whether the growing season water balance could be manipulated through planting geometry.

Methods   The effects of row spacing, row direction, and plant population on the water use, light interception, and growth or grain sorghum [*Sorghum bicolor* (L.) Moench] were investigated at Bushland, TX, on a Pullman clay loam (fine, mixed, thermic Torrertic Paleustoll).

Results   In 1983, which had a dry growing season, narrow-row spacing and higher population increased seasonal evapotranspiration (ET) by 7 and 9%, respectively, and shifted the partitioning of ET to the vegetative period. Medium population crops yielded 6.2 and 2.3 Mg/ha of dry matter and grain, respectively. High population resulted in high dry matter (6.1 Mg/ha) and low grain yield (1.6 Mg/ha), whereas low population resulted in low dry matter (5.4 Mg/ha) and high grain yield (2.3 Mg/ha). Row direction did not affect water use or yield. In 1984, dry matter production for a given amount of ET and light interception was higher in the narrow-row crops. Evapotranspiration was less for a given amount of light interception in the narrow-row crops and in the north-south row crops.

Conclusions   Narrow-row planting geometry appears to increase the partitioning of ET to the transpiration component and may improve the efficiency of dryland cropping systems.

Introduction

The article should begin by clearly identifying its subject. The author should state early the hypothesis or definition of the problem the research was designed to solve. A reader is given orientation to the research being reported by brief reference to previous concepts and research. References to literature should be limited to information that is essential to the reader's orientation. Most readers do not need long literature reviews, especially of old references if newer ones are available, or to be convinced about the importance of the research. The purpose of the introduction is to supply sufficient background information to allow the reader to understand and evaluate the results of the present study without needing to refer to previous publications on the topic.

Introductions should be short and include:

1. A brief statement of the problem that justifies doing the work, or the hypothesis on which it is based.
2. The findings of others that will be challenged or developed.
3. An explanation of the general approach and objectives. This part may indicate the means by which the question was examined, especially if the methods are new.

Materials and Methods

The purpose of this section is to give enough detail so that a competent scientist can repeat the experiments.

For materials, the authors should supply the appropriate technical specifications and quantities and source or method of preparation. If a commercially available product is used, give the name and address of its manufacturer parenthetically after the first mention of that product. If necessary the pertinent chemical and physical properties of the reagents should be listed. Chemical rather than trade names are preferred. Any plants, soils, animals and other organisms not mentioned in the abstract should be identified accurately by genus, species, cultivar, soil taxonomy, and special characteristics.

Methods should be cited by a reference if possible. If the techniques are widely familiar, use only their names. If a method is modified, an outline of the modification should be given unless the modification is trivial. Give details of unusual experimental designs or statistical methods. This section may be arranged chronologically, by a succession of techniques, or in another manner.

This section may include tables and figures.

Results

A common fault in the results section is to repeat in prose what is already clear from a cursory examination of the graphics. If the tables and figures are well constructed, they will show both the results and the experimental design.

Tables, graphs, and other illustrations in the results section should provide a clear understanding of representative data obtained from the experiments. Data included in illustrations and tables should not be extensively discussed in the text, but significant findings should be noted. When only a few determinations are presented, they should be treated descriptively in the text. Repetitive determinations should be presented in tables or graphs.

The objective of each experiment should be made clear in the text. Call attention to special features, e.g., one quantity being greater than another, one result is linear across a range, or the optimum value, etc.

Finally, the results should be connected to one another. Frequently this causes the results section to be combined with the discussion section.

Discussion

The discussion section interprets data presented in the results section, giving particular attention to the problem, question, or hypothesis presented in the introduction. A good discussion will contain:

1. Principles, relationships, and generalizations that can be supported by the results.
2. Exceptions, lack or correlation, and definition of unsettled points—gap areas or areas needing further investigation.
3. Emphasis on results and conclusions that agree or disagree with other work.
4. Practical as well as theoretical implications.
5. Conclusions, with summary of evidence for each one.

The discussion section, if not combined with the results section, should not recapitulate results, but should discuss the meaning of the results. The reader should be told how the results provide a solution to the problem stated in the introduction or given as the objective of the work. The work should be connected with previous work, with an explanation of how and why it differs or agrees. References should be limited to those that are most pertinent. Older references should be omitted if they have been superceded by more recent ones.

Speculation is encouraged but should be reasonable; firmly founded in observation and subject to tests. It must also be identified apart from the discussion and conclusion. Where results differ from previous results for unexplained reasons, possible explanations should not be labored. Controversial issues should be discussed clearly and fairly.

A common fault of discussion sections is a tendency toward too much contemplation of nonessentials. Only discussion that illuminates significant areas should be presented.

Some papers may warrant a separate conclusions section, while in other papers it is desirable to present conclusions as part of the discussion section. The latter would be a paper of average complexity where conclusions are few. Whether this section is combined or separate, the author should include any significant conclusions that have been drawn from the work. These conclusions should be carefully worded so the readers can identify and understand them.

References

The references section lists the literature cited in the paper. Authors are encouraged to cite only published, significant, and up-to-date references in their papers. This section is discussed later in more detail.

Tables and Figures

Supporting data are usually presented in tables and figures. Chapter 6 in this manual contains a discussion on their preparation.

MANUSCRIPTS SUBMITTED FOR OTHER SOCIETY PUBLICATIONS

Journal article format is usually not used in other publications of the societies, but certain sections, such as references, follow the conventions established for the journal article. Other sections, such as discussion, may be called something else in book chapters, etc., but should adhere to the same scientific and editorial requirements as journal articles.

DETAILS OF MANUSCRIPT PREPARATION

Typing

The manuscript must be typed double spaced on good grade, 216- by 280-mm (8.5- by 11-inch) paper, or prepared by other techniques to obtain a copy providing comparable quality. Manuscripts produced by word processor printers are acceptable only if they are of good legible quality. The printer should have true subscripts and superscripts rather than compressed ones. Print should be as dark as that produced by good-quality typewriters with dark ribbons. Letters should be completely formed and even on a line to avoid distortion.

Manuscripts must be on line-numbered paper. Line-numbered paper is supplied free to authors of book and monograph chapters and may be purchased by others from headquarters office. Other line numbering can also be used, e.g., with a word processor. Submit as many copies of the manuscript as required by the publication; for journals, this number is four. All copies must be legible throughout. Photocopies are acceptable if they are as legible as the original. Authors should keep a file copy of their manuscript. Other guidelines are as follows:

1. Double space all typing, including footnotes, references, data in tables, and captions to figures and tables. Use only one side of the sheet. Indent each paragraph five spaces.

2. When revising a manuscript, type a correction or addition of a few words between lines on the original page. For major revisions, retype the paragraphs or pages involved. Deletion of a word or two should be clearly marked on the original pages. If a manuscript is retyped during the review-revision process, the original copy must be returned along with the revised one.

Estimating Length of Journal Articles and Book Chapter

About four manuscript pages of elite typescript (12-pitch face) occupy one printed journal page; two manuscript pages equal one printed book page. One elite typescript page should contain 25 lines 150 mm (6 inches) wide. If the manuscript is typed with pica (10-pitch face) or some other size of type and another length of line, the proportions will vary accordingly.

The ratio of manuscript to printed page of other publications varies, and editors should be consulted about the format requirements.

Space required for figures can be estimated from the size of the originals and the amount of reduction (usually 40 to 60%) that will be made in preparing negatives and photostats for printing.

Space required for tables can be estimated from the number of lines of headings, subheadings, and numbers in the table. Ten lines require about 25 mm (1 inch) of column space. If the lines contain more than 60 numbers or letters, the table will be set two columns wide.

Headings and Subheadings

Authors should examine samples of the publication for which the manuscript is being prepared. For full-length journal papers, the main text headings, such as Materials and Methods, are typed in capitals in the center of the line. Secondary center headings and side headings are typed in capitals and lower case letters. Run-in headings are typed in the normal paragraph position and underscored for printing in italics. Use of subheadings can help divide papers for guiding readers, but excessive use is distracting. Keep subheadings short.

Captions

Figure captions must be typed together on a separate page. Use "Fig." for abbreviation in captions. Table headings must be typed along with the table and do not require a separate page. Number the figure caption page to follow the reference list.

Footnotes

Authors should avoid the use of footnotes. A necessary footnote in the text may be a government disclaimer in reference to a named commercial product or a mentioned trade name.

References

In all society publications, only literature that is available through libraries can be cited. Material not available through libraries, such as personal communications or unpublished data, should be given in text as parenthetical matter. (Material submitted to but not accepted by a journal or other publication is considered to be unpublished data.) Include the source of data and the date (e.g., R.D. Jackson, 1987, personal communication). Authors are encouraged to cite only significant, published references. Abstracts, theses or dissertations, and secondary materials should be carefully examined by authors before including them in the reference section. Many of these materials are later published in sources that are more easily obtained by readers. If possible, authors should cite the more accessible source of these contributions.

Two sources of error occur in reference citation: inaccurate copying of the bibliographic information and compilation of the reference section after the paper is written. Reviewers and editors cannot be expected to verify the accuracy of the literature citations.

Authors, when copying the publication data from a document, should verify their final product against the document. The reference's author name, title, and other parts should exactly match that shown on the original document. When in doubt, the author should consult a reference librarian for the correct bibliographic citation of difficult material. Readers should be able to obtain cited references by presenting the list to a librarian.

The second type of error occurs when authors either (i) do not include a reference cited in the manuscript or have omitted a reference from the text and have left it in the reference list, or (ii) the names and dates in the reference list do not agree with those in the text. Authors are urged to check the alphabetical reference list against the citations in the body of the manuscript before submitting the manuscript for publication.

Two methods of giving references in the text are acceptable: the name-year system (e.g., Smith, 1987; CSSA, 1988) and the reference number method (e.g., 3). For two authors, name both: Jones and Johnson (1987). With three or more authors, use et al.: Smith et al. (1987) or Smith et al. (9). For two or more articles by the same author(s) in the same year, designate them as follows: Brown (1987a,b) or Smith et al. (1987a,b).

Each reference to a periodical publication must include, in order, the author(s), year of publication, full title of the article, publication in which it appears, and volume and inclusive page numbers. (See examples later in this chapter.)

Reference to a book, bulletin, government document, or conference proceedings must give the author(s), year, title, name of editor(s) if appropriate, edition if other than the first, location and dates (if applicable), publisher, city of publication, and number of the volume (if two or more). If specific pages in a book (not entire chapters) are cited, mention them in the text: Weisman (1983, p. 75).

Publications without consecutive pagination (i.e., each issue within the volume begins with page 1) should include the issue number: 11(2)5–10.

Arrange the list alphabetically by the surnames of authors. Two or more articles by the same author (or authors) are listed chronologically; two or more in the same year are indicated by the letters, a,b,c, etc. All single-authored articles of a given individual should precede multiple-author articles of which the individual is senior author. Entries with the same senior author (e.g., Shotwell below) should be organized by alphabetizing surnames of succeeding coauthors and then by year, when the name is repeated exactly (see entries 3 and 4 below).

1. Shotwell , O.L. 1984. _____.
2. Shotwell, O.L., M.L. Goulden, and C.W. Hesseltine. 1982. _____.
3. Shotwell, O.L., C.W. Hesseltine, and M.L. Goulden. 1983. _____.
4. Shotwell, O.L., C.W. Hesseltine, and M.L. Goulden. 1984. _____.
5. Shotwell, O.L., C.W. Hesseltine, E.E. Vandegraft, and M.L. Goulden. 1983. _____.
6. Shotwell, O.L., W.F. Kwolek, M.L. Goulden, L.K. Jackson, and C.W. Hesseltine. 1981. _____.
7. Shotwell, O.L., and D.W. Zwieg. 1984. _____.

Do not capitalize the titles of articles, bulletins, or books except proper names and the first letter of the first word of the title. (See below for examples of literature references.)

Use acronyms or commonly understood abbreviations for organizations; e.g., ASA, TVA, ICRISAT, U.S. Gov. Print. Office when used as publishers, or for the text reference. Spell them out when they are used as authors. Do not abbreviate state names except after a city name such as Madison, WI; then use zip code abbreviations.

Periodical titles should be abbreviated as given in *Chemical Abstracts Service Source Index* (Chem. Abstr. Serv., 1984).

Dissertations that are available on microfilm or in abstract form have a number and publication data that must be given in the reference. If available, please supply the dissertation abstract number or the University Microfilm number.

Consult the *CBE Style Manual* for examples of the various types of references. Some common types are shown below.

Standard Journal Article

Griffis, C.L., D.W. Ritter, and E.J. Matthews. 1983. Simulation of rotary spreader distribution patterns. Trans. ASAE 26:33–37.

Book

Donahue, R.L., R.W. Miller, and J.C. Shickluna. 1983. Soils: An introduction to soils and plant growth. 5th ed. Prentice-Hall, Englewood Cliffs, NJ.

Chapter in Book

Moss, J.P., I.V. Spielman, A.P. Burge, A.K. Singh, and R.W. Gibbons. 1981. Utilization of wild *Arachis* species as a source of *Cercospora* leafspot resistance in groundnut breeding. p. 673–677. *In* G.K. Manna and U. Sinhu (ed.) Perspectives in cytology and genetics. Vol. 3. Hindasia Publ., Delhi, India.

Article With No Identifiable Author

Avoid use if possible.

Anonymous. 1984. Computer programs from your radio? Agri-Marketing 22(6):66.

General Magazine Article

Davenport, C.H. 1981. Sowing the seeds. Barron's. 2 March, p. 10.

Mulvaney, D.L., and L. Paul. 1984. Rotating crops and tillage. Crops Soils 36(7):18–19.

Technical Report

U.S. Environmental Protection Agency. 1981. Process design manual for land treatment of municipal wastewater. USEPA Rep. 625/1-77-008 (COE EM1110-1-501). U.S. Gov. Print. Office, Washington DC.

Conference, Symposium, or Workshop Proceedings

Include page numbers, editor(s), title, location and dates, and publisher's name and location.

Uehara, G., B.B. Trangmar, and R.S. Yost. 1985. Spatial variability of soil properties. p. 61–95. *In* D.R. Nielsen and J. Bouma (ed.) Soil spatial variability. Proc. Workshop ISSS and SSSA, Las Vegas, NV. 30 Nov.–1 Dec. 1984. PUDOC, Wageningen, Netherlands.

Dissertation

Reeder, J.D. 1981. Nitrogen transformation in revegetated coal spoils. Ph.D. diss. Colorado State Univ., Fort Collins (Diss. Abstr. 81-26447).

Transactions

Jansson, S.L. 1967. Soil organic matter and fertility. p. 1–10. *In* G.V. Jacks (ed.) Soil chemistry and fertility. Trans. Jt. Meet. Comm. 2, 4, Int. Soc. Soil Sci. 1966. Univ. Press, Aberdeen, Scotland.

Translation

Vigerust, E., and A.R. Selmer-Olsen. 1981. Uptake of heavy metals by some plants from sewage sludge. (In Norwegian.) Fast Avfall. 2:26–29.

Advances in Agronomy Series

Savant, N.K., and S.K. DeDatta. 1982. Nitrogen transformations in wetland rice soils. Adv. Agron. 35:241–302.

Patent

Titcomb, S.T., and A.A. Juers. 1976. Reduced calorie bread and method of making same. U.S. Patent 3 979 523. Date issued: 7 September.

Miscellaneous Publication

Wadleigh, C.H. 1968. Wastes in relation to agriculture and forestry. USDA Misc. Publ. 1065. U.S. Gov. Print. Office, Washington, DC.

Corporate Author of Article

American Public Health Association. 1980. Standard methods for the examination of wastewater. 15th ed. Am. Public Health Assoc., New York.

State Publication

DePuit, E.J., C.J. Skilbred, and J.G. Coenenberg. 1980. Vegetation characteristics on sodic mine spoils. p. 48–74. *In* D.J. Dollhopf et al. (ed.) Chemical amendments and irrigation effects on sodium migration and vegetation characteristics on sodic mine soils in Montana. Montana Agric. Exp. Stn. Bull. 736.

Federal Publication

Soil Survey Staff. 1975. Soil taxonomy: A basic system of soil classification for making and interpreting soil surveys. USDA-SCS Agric. Handb. 436. U.S. Gov. Print. Office, Washington, DC.

Society Publications

Journals

Allen, S.G., G.A. Taylor, and J.M. Martin. 1986. Agronomic characterization of 'Yogo' hard red winter wheat plant height isolines. Agron. J. 78:63–66.

Monographs

Thompson, J.F., I.K. Smith, and J.T. Madison. 1986. Sulfur metabolism in plants. *In* M.A. Tabatabai (ed.) Sulfur in agriculture. Agronomy 27:57–121.

Blake, G.R., and K.H. Hartge. 1986. Particle density. *In* A. Klute (ed.) Methods of soil analysis. Part 1. 2nd ed. Agronomy 9:377–382.

Books

Achorn, F.P., and H.L. Balay. 1985. Developments in potassium fertilizer technology. p. 49–66. *In* R.D. Munson (ed.) Potassium in agriculture. ASA, CSSA, and SSSA, Madison, WI.

Special Publications

McMichael, B.L., and H.M. Taylor. 1987. Applications and limitations of rhizotrons and minirhizotrons. p.. 1–13. *In* H.M. Taylor (ed.) Minirhizotron observation tubes: Methods and applications for measuring rhizosphere dynamics. ASA Spec. Publ. 50. ASA, CSSA, and SSSA, Madison, WI.

Agronomy Abstracts

Campbell, G.S. 1987. Simulation of water uptake by plant roots. p. 10. *In* Agronomy abstracts. ASA, Madison, WI.

Chapter 5. Conventions and Style

Authors are responsible for making papers clear, concise, and accurate. Manuscripts should be thoroughly reviewed by the author's colleagues before submission to the society. Authors should consult this manual, other society guidelines and instructions mentioned here, and general style manuals when preparing material. Manuscripts that are not properly prepared are returned to authors for corrections.

Helpful sources for authors of journal articles, monographs, books, special publications, and other publications of the societies are the *CBE Style Manual, The Chicago Manual of Style, U.S. Government Printing Office Style Manual* and other widely available publications. These books contain details of grammar, punctuation, table preparation, and other style matters. Authors are also encouraged to study recent issues of society journals and books for the general style and format used.

This manual should be used as a primary source for conventions and style. Other books, such as the ones listed above, supplement this manual.

NOMENCLATURE AND TERMINOLOGY

Biology

The common name, Latin binomial or trinomial (in italics), and the authority should be shown for plants, insects, animals, and pathogens when first mentioned. If the first mention is in the abstract, they do not need to be repeated in the text. Common names, if they exist, should be used in titles without the scientific names. Common crop names should not end in the letter "s" (e.g., "oat," not "oats"; "pea," not "peas"; "soybean," not "soybeans," etc.).

Scientific names should be in accordance with published authorities. For cultivated plants, the rules of nomenclature have been established in the *International Code of Nomenclature for Cultivated Plants* (Brickell, 1980). Various publications, e.g., *Hortus III*, record these names, but revisions are

33

made from time to time because of new taxonomic and nomenclatural evidence. *Crop Science* publishes articles on registered cultivars, germplasms, parental lines, and genetic stocks. Crop cultivars (not experimental lines and strains) must be identified by single quotation marks when first mentioned in the abstract or text, e.g., 'Vernal' alfalfa (*Medicago sativa* L.) or *Medicago sativa* L. 'Vernal'. All authorities including secondary ones, should be cited; e.g., *Glycine max* (L.) Merr. Do not use the word cultivar and single quotation marks at the same time. The abbreviation "cv." (for cultivars) is allowed in the societies' publications. The abbreviation "var." (for varieties) refers to botanical varieties and is not considered appropriate for cultivars. The terms cultivar and variety are synonymous for cultivated plants, but the term cultivar is preferred.

The Crop Science Society of America, through its committee on crop registration, publishes lists of registered field crop cultivars. *Registered Field Crop Varieties: 1926–1981* (CSSA, 1982) is available from the headquarters office. Registrations of cultivars, germplasms, and parental lines subsequent to this list are published with the annual index of *Crop Science*, beginning in 1986, with the 1982–1985 accumulation in the July-August 1987 issue of the journal. Registrations of genetic stocks began in 1988.

Chemistry

Chemical symbols should be used instead of words for elements, ions or compounds except at the beginning of a sentence. These symbols do not have to be defined the first time that they are used. Where the representation is general and the chemical species is not specified, the ionic charge should not be used; e.g., Ca, Fe, K, NH_4, NO_3, SO_4, and PO_4. Use ionic notation in systems where the dominant reaction is electrostatic (as in cation exchange, K^+), or where the author might have used the word "ion." If the word "ion" is used after a chemical species, it is not necessary to include its ionic charge. Where the oxidation state is not obvious in a formula or where the oxidation state is known and is important, it should be specified; e.g., Fe(II).

The amounts and proportions of fertilizer nutrient elements must be expressed in terms of the elements or in other ways as needed for theoretical purposes. The amounts or proportions of the oxide forms (P_2O_5, K_2O, etc.) may also be included, in parentheses.

Full chemical names for compounds must be used when they are first mentioned in the abstract or text. If given in the abstract, full chemical names do not need to be repeated in the text. Use the most up-to-date chemical names available. The names can be carried in tabular form if there are a large number of them. Thereafter, the common or generic name can be used, e.g., atrazine, 2,4-D, etc. Trade names should be avoided whenever possible. If it is necessary to use a trade name, it should be capitalized and spelled out as specified by the trademark owner.

In the USA and Canada the authority for names of chemical compounds is *Chemical Abstracts* and its indexes. The American Chemical Society's

The ACS Style Guide (Dodd, 1986) and the *CBE Style Manual* contain many additional details on nomenclature in chemistry and biochemistry. Publications of the American Chemical Society's committee on nomenclature, and the nomenclature commissions of the International Union of Pure and Applied Chemistry (IUPAC) are available through Chemical Abstracts Service, Columbus, OH.

The section on SI units in this chapter has further information regarding units and concentration.

Information on pesticides is found in *Farm Chemicals Handbook* (Meister Publ. Co., current ed.).

Many of the organic substances used for pesticides contain prefixes, letters, and numbers designating configuration and rotation of the chemical structure. Some general rules are:

1. The most common hyphenated prefixes that should be italicized (underlined) are *o*-, *m*-, *p*-, *s*-, *cis*-, *trans*-, *sec*-, *tert*- *endo*-, and *exo*-. The prefixes bis- and tris- are not italicized. Elements that occur as locants are also italicized: *O*-, *S*-, *N*-, *H*-, etc.

2. Configurational relationships may be indicated by the italic capital letter prefix *R* and *S*. Rotation may be shown with small capitals D and L. In some cases the italicized lower case *d* and *l* are used.

SPECIALIZED TERMINOLOGY

Professional societies in special fields and the *CBE Style Manual* list terms used in various disciplines. Authors using specialized vocabulary not in material published by those societies or in a good dictionary should consult those societies before establishing new terminology. Committees of ASA, CSSA, and SSSA have studied terminology in specialized fields and have indicated a preference in many cases.

Crop Science Terminology

A complete *Glossary of Crop Science Terms* will be published in late 1988 (CSSA, 1988). Earlier lists of terms compiled by various committees on crop terminology were published in *Crop Science* (Leonard et al., 1968; Shibles, 1976). Their reports cite the relevant articles and lists published in related fields and include the previously published reports issued as mimeographs or articles on definitions by the earlier committees. In addition, letters in the journal comment on various aspects of terminology (e.g., Dybing, 1977).

Soil Science Terminology

The *Glossary of Soil Science Terms* (SSSA, 1987) contains definitions of nearly 1400 terms, plus appendices covering obsolete terms, a procedural guide for tillage terminology, and new designations for soil horizons and layers.

Soil Identification

All soils discussed in publications of the three societies should be identified according to the U.S. soil taxonomic system the first time each soil is mentioned. Taxonomic identification given in the abstract does not have to be repeated in the text. If possible, give the series name in addition to the family name. If the series name is not known, give the family name. If the family name is not known, give the subgroup or a higher category name.

Use the singular form if the reference is to a single pedon or polypedon or to a single class. Use the plural form in reference to several or all of the soils (polypedons) of a class. Anything less than a pedon, such as a single horizon, is only part of a soil. Bodies of soil less than a full pedon are considered as samples of soil or as soil material. Use the present tense if the soil still exists or reasonably is thought to still exist. Examples are as follows:

> The soil material used in this study was collected from the A horizon of a Brookston pedon (a fine-loamy, mixed, mesic Typic Argiaquoll).
>
> A Cisne soil, fine, montmorillonitic, mesic Mollic Albaqualf, was described and sampled at this site.
>
> Criteria for the Typic Hapludult subgroup were examined.
>
> Ontario soils, in the fine-loamy, mixed, mesic Glossoboric Hapludalf family, were studied in greater detail.
>
> Soils of the Ramona series (fine-loamy, mixed, thermic Typic Haploxeralfs) were treated.
>
> All soils used in the experiments are Typic Dystrochrepts.

For field experiments, the soil present in the plots or fields should be identified, preferably as phases of soil series so that surface texture and slope are known in addition to profile properties. Any dissimilar inclusions that are present also should be named and their extent suggested. It also may be appropriate to name and briefly describe the common soils of the area surrounding the study site. For example:

> The 5-ha study area is mapped as Yolo silt loam, 0 to 2% slopes. The Yolo soils are fine-silty, mixed, nonacid, thermic Typic Xerorthents. Small areas of Cortina very gravely sandy loam soils (loamy-skeletal, mixed, nonacid, thermic Typic Xerofluvents) occupy about 10% of the study area.

Revisions of the U.S. system of soil taxonomy (Soil Survey Staff, 1975) have been issued in the *National Soil Taxonomy Handbook* (U.S. Department of Agriculture, 1982-1986) and in *Keys to Soil Taxonomy* (Soil Management Support Services, 1985. Additional issues of the handbook and new versions of the Keys are expected. If possible, consult with members of the National Cooperative Soil Survey (NCSS) and check the current NCSS soil classification file for proper identification. The USDA-SCS soil horizon designations (Guthrie and Witty, 1982) should be used for nomenclature of soil horizons.

Contributors outside the USA are encouraged to give soil identification according to the U.S. soil taxonomy in addition to the identification in their national system.

Light Measurements and Photosynthesis

The term "light intensity" to denote the amount of light incident on a surface (Dybing, 1977) has been abandoned. The *Crop Science* editorial board has also discontinued the use of the photometric system and units scaled to the response of the human eye. Society publications use the radiometric system with SI units denoting the energy or the quantum content of the radiation used by plants.

Terms recommended by the Committee on Crop Terminology for the expression of photosynthetic energy and photosynthetic capacity were defined by Shibles (1976). These terms are "photosynthetically active radiation," "photosynthetic photon flux density," "photosynthetic irradiance," "apparent photosynthesis," and "CO_2 exchange rate."

STATISTICAL ANALYSIS AND EXPERIMENTAL DESIGN

Readers of scientific publications must understand how the authors designed and conducted their experiments so that the results can be judged for validity and so that previous experiments may serve as a basis for the design of future experiments. Research design consists of two components: treatment design and experimental or environmental design. Both of these components must be explicitly described when reporting results of experiments in the societies' publications.

Treatment design is used in a broad sense and includes levels of factors in factorial experiments, populations of genotypes used in genetic and physiological experiments, soil types, and many other physical and biological variables. Experimental design refers to the method of arranging the experimental units and the method of assigning treatments to the units. Included should be the number of replicates, a description of conditions at field sites and in greenhouse or controlled environment chambers, the number of sites and years, and how measurements were made for specific traits. Blocking or other restrictions used in assigning treatments to experimental units should be clearly described. The number of experimental units used and the number of samples taken from each unit should also be clear to the reader.

Special care should be taken in reporting the results of field research. First, the results must be obtained using adequate treatment and experimental design, and, as indicated previously, the treatment and design should be clearly described. Second, because field conditions are not repeatable from year to year or site to site, an adequate sample of environments must be used. Usually studies on crop characteristics that are sensitive to environmental effects must be repeated to establish the validity of results. This may be done by using other sites, years, or growth periods within a year. Depending on the nature of the study, two or more environmental regimes may be necessary to obtain meaningful results.

A complete description of tillage and planting implements, including model numbers, can greatly assist in the understanding of research in areas such as soil management and chemical incorporation. Information of use includes depth and speed of operation as well as type of ground-engaging tool.

The experimental and treatment designs dictate the proper method of statistical analysis and the basis for assessing the precision of treatment means.

A measure of the precision achieved should be reported for all data on which conclusions are drawn. Two methods for doing this include reporting the standard error of a treatment mean or the coefficient of variation. It is not usually necessary to report standard deviations for individual portions of the total experiment.

When treatments have a logical structure, orthogonal contrasts among treatments means should be made. All possible comparisons among treatment means can be done, but authors should be aware of the limitations of this approach when little information exists on the structure of the treatment (Carmer and Walker, 1982; Chew, 1976; Little 1978; Nelson and Rawlings, 1983; Peterson, 1977).

When common experimental designs such as the completely randomized, randomized block, or split-plot designs are used, it is not necessary to cite a reference, but the author should identify the design. It is appropriate, however, to cite references to little-used methods, designs, or statistical analyses. Also, if computer programs are used that are not commonly used, the documentation reference should be cited.

Table 1. Some abbreviations widely used in statistics.†

| Statistic | Sample | | Population |
	Preferred symbol	Acceptable symbol	
Arithmetic mean	$\bar{x}$		μ
Chi-square	χ^2		
Correlation coefficient	r		
Coefficient of multiple determination	R^2		
Coefficient of simple determination	r^2		
Coefficient of variation	CV		
Degrees of freedom	df	DF	
Least significant difference	LSD		
Multiple correlation coefficient	R		
Not significant	NS		
Probability of type I error	α		
Probability of type II error	β		
Regression coefficient	b		β
Sample size	n		N
Standard error of mean	SE	$s_{\bar{x}}$	$\sigma_{\bar{x}}$
Standard deviation of sample	SD	s	σ
Student's t	t		
Variance	s^2		σ^2
Variance ratio	F		

† The symbols *, **, and *** are used to show significance at the $P = 0.05$, 0.01, and 0.001 levels, respectively. Significance at other levels should be designated by a supplemental note.

Brief analyses of variance (ANOVA) tables with mean squares and degrees of freedom may be published in instances where they are needed for clarity in reporting results. For factorial experiments or for treatments where treatment structure suggests logical contrasts, these tables are an efficient way to summarize the relative importance of the various effects, especially if imbalance in the design was caused by unequal replication. Analyses of variance tables are also useful in reporting mean squares in situations where variance component estimation is the principle objective. In such instances, factors considered to be fixed and those considered to be random should be designated.

Some widely used statistical abbreviations and symbols are given in Table 1. Additional guidelines may be published by the various journals.

MEASUREMENTS, SI SYSTEM

The SI system (le Système International d'Unités) of reporting measurements is required in all society publications except *Journal of Production Agriculture* and *Agronomy News*. Other units may be reported in parentheses at the option of the author if this inclusion will clarify interpretation of the data.

Basic references on the use of SI units were published by the National Bureau of Standards and the American Society for Testing and Materials. The 1981 issue of *Journal of Agronomic Education* contains three articles on the use of SI units. Although the articles are useful, recent conversion tables are more accurate (see Table 7 in this section).

Base, Supplementary, and Derived Units

The SI system is based on seven base and two supplementary units that are listed in Table 2 with their names and symbols.

The definition of the mole (mol), adopted by the 14th General Conference on Weights and Measures in 1971, is the amount of substance of a system that contains as many elementary elements as there are atoms in 12 g of ^{12}C. When the unit mole is used, the entities must be specified.

Table 2. Base and supplementary SI units.

Quantity	Unit	Symbol
Amount of substance	mole	mol
Electric current	ampere	A
Length	meter	m
Luminous intensity	candela	cd
Mass	kilogram	kg
Thermodynamic temperature	kelvin	K
Time	second	s
Plane angle	radian	rad
Solid angle	steradian	sr

Table 3. Derived SI units with special names.

Quantity	Name	Symbol	Expression in terms of other units	Expression in terms of SI base units
Absorbed dose, specific energy imparted, kerma, absorbed dose index	gray	Gy	J/kg	$m^2\ s^{-2}$
Activity (of a radionuclide)	becquerel	Bq		s^{-1}
Capacitance	farad	F	C/V	$m^{-2}\ kg^{-1}\ s^4\ A^2$
Celsius temperature	degree Celsius	°C		K
Conductance	siemens	S	A/V	$m^{-2}\ kg^{-1}\ s^3\ A^2$
Electric potential, potential difference, electromotive force	volt	V	W/A	$m^2\ kg\ s^{-3}\ A^{-1}$
Electric resistance	ohm	Ω	V/A	$m^2\ kg\ s^{-3}\ A^{-2}$
Energy, work, quantity of heat	joule	J	Nm	$m^2\ kg\ s^{-2}$
Force	newton	N		$m\ kg\ s^{-2}$
Frequency	hertz	Hz		s^{-1}
Power, radiant flux	watt	W	J/s	$m^2\ kg\ s^{-3}$
Pressure, stress	pascal	Pa	N/m²	$m^{-1}\ kg\ s^{-2}$
Quantity of electricity, electric charge	coulomb	C		s A

Derived units (Table 3) are expressed algebraically in terms of base units. Some of these units have been given special names and symbols, which may be used to express still other derived units. An example of a derived unit with a special name is the newton (N) for force. The newton is expressed in basic units as meter kilogram per second squared. Another unit with a special name is the pascal (Pa), which is a newton per square meter.

The SI base unit for thermodynamic temperature is kelvin (K). Because of its wide use, the Celsius scale may also be used to express temperature. The degree sign should be used with Celsius temperature (°C) but not with the kelvin scale.

Using SI Units

The prefixes and symbols listed in Table 4 are used to indicate orders of magnitude in SI units. They reduce the use of nonsignificant digits and decimals and provide a convenient substitute for writing powers of 10 as generally preferred in computations. With some exceptions (see Use of Non-SI Units Section) base units (kg, m, s) are required in the denominator of combinations of units, while appropriate prefixes for multiples (or submultiples) are selected for the numerator so that the numerical value of the term lies between 0.1 and 1000. Therefore, numerical values can be written without having to show that the data were multiplied by a given factor to obtain the unit presented. For example, a value of 0.015 kg ha^{-1} should be reported as 15 g ha^{-1} rather than 1.5 kg ha^{-1} ($\times\ 10^{-2}$). An exponent attached to a sym-

Table 4. SI prefixes.

Order of magnitude	Prefix	Symbol
10^{18}	exa	E
10^{15}	peta	P
10^{12}	tera	T
10^{9}	giga	G
10^{6}	mega	M
10^{3}	kilo	k
10^{2}	hecto†	h†
10^{1}	deca‡	da‡
10^{-1}	deci†	d†
10^{-2}	centi†	c†
10^{-3}	milli	m
10^{-6}	micro	μ
10^{-9}	nano	n
10^{-12}	pico	p
10^{-15}	femto	τ
10^{-18}	atto	a

† To be avoided when possible.   ‡ Not to be used.

bol containing a prefix indicates that the unit with its prefix is raised to the power expressed by the exponent; e.g.,

$$1 \text{ mm}^3 = (10^{-3} \text{ m})^3 = 10^{-9} \text{ m}^3.$$

Punctuation is used sparingly with SI units. The center dot, generally used to indicate the product of two or more units, is omitted when there is no risk of confusion with another unit symbol (use N m not N•m). A solidus (oblique stroke,/), a horizontal line, or negative powers may be used to express a derived unit formed from two others by division; e.g.,

$$\text{m/s or m s}^{-1}.$$

Only one solidus may be used in combinations of units, unless parentheses are used to avoid ambiguity, e.g.,

$$\text{g m}^{-2} \text{ s}^{-1} \text{ or g/(m}^2 \text{ s) but not g/m}^2\text{/s.}$$

Periods are not used after any SI unit symbol except at the end of a sentence. When numbers are less than one, a zero should be written before the decimal marker (e.g., 0.7).

Use of Non-SI Units

Some units not in SI can be used—including use in the denominator—in the societies' publications, but these units have been limited to those that are convenient for crop and soil scientists. The quantity of area can be expressed as hectare (1 ha = 10^4 m^2). The use of liter (1 L = 10^{-3} m^3) in the denominator of derived units is permitted, but m^3 is encouraged. The use of centimeter (cm) is acceptable for short measurements such as plant height, row width, soil depth, etc. Soil bulk density can be expressed as g cm^{-3}, but Mg or t m^{-3} is encouraged. Angstroms are allowed for crystalline spacing, and wave number can be reported as cm^{-1}.

The base unit second (s) is the preferred unit of time. Other units— minute (min), hour (h), day (d), week (wk), and year (yr)—are acceptable although their use often introduces difficulties in rapid conversion from one time scale to another. Units of time that vary in length, e.g., month, should not be used. One allowable exception is when climatic data are given for specifically named months in the text, tables, or figures (e.g., Average July rainfall for the test area is 52 mm.).

In SI, a tonne (t) equals 10^3 kg, or 1 Mg, and is understood to be a metric ton. Do not use the term "metric ton." When expressing yields or application rates, the terms t ha^{-1} or Mg ha^{-1} are both acceptable, although t ha^{-1} is the more widely used term. Teragram (Tg) should be used in place of million tonnes where applicable.

Radians is the base unit for measurement of plane angles, but degrees are also acceptable.

Specific Applications

Special attention is required for reporting concentration, exchange composition and capacity, energy of soil water (or water potential), and light. Table 5 summarizes the appropriate units for society publications. Prefixes, other than those shown in Table 5, may be used as noted in Table 4, so that numerical values are between 0.1 and 1000.

Concentration

Normality, N, the amount of substance concentration based on the concept of equivalent concentration, should not be used. Concentrations should be expressed on a molar basis as shown below. Examples for correctly expressing concentration (conc.) include:

$$\text{conc. (HCl)} = 0.1 \text{ mol L}^{-1} = 0.1 \; M \text{ HCl and}$$

$$\text{conc. (H}_3\text{PO}_4) = 2.1 \text{ mol m}^{-3} = 2.1 \text{ mmol L}^{-1} = 2.1 \text{ m}M \text{ H}_3\text{PO}_4.$$

The concentration 0.1 mol L^{-1} can also be reported as a 0.1 M (molar) solution. Solutions containing ions of mixed valence also should be given on a molar basis of each ion. Molality (mol kg^{-1}) is an acceptable term and unit; it is the preferred unit for precise, nonisothermal conditions.

Gas concentration can be expressed as mol m^{-3}, g m^{-3} partial pressure, or mole fraction. The denominator of the mole fraction needs no summation sign because SI defines a mole as Avogadro's number of any defined substance, including a mixture such as air. An O_2 concentration of 210 mL L^{-1} is therefore 21×10^{-2} mol mol^{-1} or 0.21 mol fraction. A CO_2 concentration of 335 μmol mol^{-1} equals 335 μmol fraction.

Table 5. Preferred (P) and acceptable (A) units for several quantities.

Quantity	Application	Unit	Symbol
Concentration	Known molar mass (liquid and solid material)	mole per cubic meter (P)	mol m^{-3}
		mole per kilogram (P)	mol kg^{-1}
		mole per liter (A)	mol L^{-1}
		gram per liter (A)	g L^{-1}
	Unknown molar mass (liquid and solid material)	gram per kilogram (P)	g kg^{-1}
		gram per cubic meter (P)	g m^{-3}
		gram per liter (A)	g L^{-1}
	Known ionic charge	mole charge per cubic meter (P)	mol$_c$ m^{-3}
		mole charge per liter (A)	mol$_c$ L^{-1}
	Gas	mole per cubic meter (P)	mol m^{-3}
		gram per cubic meter (A)	g m^{-3}
		gram per liter (A)	g L^{-1}
		liter per liter (A)	L L^{-1}
		microliter per liter (A)	μL L^{-1}
		mole per liter (A)	mol L^{-1}
		mole fraction (A)	mol mol^{-1}
Exchange parameters	Exchange capacity	mole charge of saturating ion per kilogram (P)	mol$_c$ kg^{-1}
		centimole charge of saturating ion per kilogram (A)	cmol$_c$ kg^{-1}
	Exchangeable ion composition	mole charge of specific ion per kilogram	mol$_c$ kg^{-1}
	Sum of exchangeable ions	mole of ion charge per kilogram	mol$_c$ kg^{-1}
Light	Irradiance	watt per square meter	W m^{-2}
	Photon flux density (400–700 nm)	micromole per square meter per second	μmol m^{-2} s^{-1}
Water potential	Driving force for flow	joule per kilogram (P)	J kg^{-1}
		kilopascal (A)	kPa
		meter of water in a gravitational field (A)	m

Nutrient concentration in plants, soil, or fertilizer can be expressed on the basis of mass as well as the amount of substance. For example, plant phosphorus concentration could be reported as 180 mmol P kg^{-1}, or 5.58 g P kg^{-1}. Extractable nutrients in soil should be expressed as mg kg^{-1} or g m^{-3} when soil is measured on a mass or volume basis, respectively. Exchangeable ions by the usual acetate procedure on weighed samples should be expressed as mmol$_c$ kg^{-1} or cmol$_c$ kg^{-1}.

Water content of plant tissue or plant parts can be expressed in terms of water mass per unit mass of plant material, e.g., g H$_2$O kg^{-1}. Authors should state whether reported plant mass is on a dry or wet basis.

Exchange Composition and Capacity

Historically, soil scientists have expressed exchange capacity in milli-equivalents (meq) per 100 g. The units in neither the numerator nor the denominator conform to SI. Exchange capacity and exchangeable ion composition should be expressed as moles of charge per kilogram, e.g., 5 cmol$_c$

kg^{-1}. Inclusion of $(+)$ or $(-)$ is not needed; it should be apparent from the text. If the cation exchange capacity is determined by the single ion saturation technique, the ion used should be specified in the text since it can affect the cation exchange capacity measured. If Mg^{2+} were used for the soil, and specific ion effects were nonsignificant, the cation exchange capacity would be expressed as 8 $cmol_c$ $(1/2\ Mg^{2+})\ kg^{-1}$.

Energy of Soil Water or Water Potential

Soil water potential refers to its equivalent potential energy; it can be expressed on either a mass or a volume basis. Energy per unit mass has units of joules per kilogram ($J\ kg^{-1}$) in SI. Energy per unit volume is dimensionally equivalent to pressure, and the SI pressure unit is the pascal (Pa). One joule per kilogram is 1 kPa if the density of water is 1 $Mg\ m^{-3}$; and since 1 bar = 100 kPa, 1 $J\ kg^{-1}$ is equal to 0.01 bar at this same density. Energy per unit mass ($J\ kg^{-1}$) is preferred over the pressure unit (Pa).

The height of a water column in the earth's gravitational field, energy per unit of weight, can be used as an index of water potential or energy. The potential in joules per kilogram ($J\ kg^{-1}$) is the gravitational constant multiplied by the height of the water column. Since the gravitational constant is essentially 10 (9.81 $m\ s^{-2}$), hydraulic head in meters of water is approximately 10 times the water potential expressed in joules per kilogram or kilopascals.

Light

Accepted SI notation for total radiant energy per unit area is joule per square meter ($J\ m^{-2}$). Energy per unit time or irradiance is expressed in watts per square meter ($W\ m^{-2}$). Alternative units, based on calories or ergs for energy and square centimeter for area, are not acceptable. Also, photometric units, e.g., lux, are not acceptable.

Plant scientists studying photochemically triggered responses, e.g., photosynthesis, photomorphogenesis, and phototropism, may quantify radiation in terms of number of photons rather than energy content. Photon flux density per unit area should be expressed in moles of photons per square meter second ($mol\ m^{-2}\ s^{-1}$). Historically, one mole (1 mol) of photons has been equated with one einstein (1 E). Thus, $\mu E\ m^{-2}\ s^{-1}$ is in common use as a unit of photon flux density but is not acceptable in SI. The SI unit μmol photon $m^{-2}\ s^{-1}$ are equivalent and should be used. The photosynthetic photon flux density (PPFD) is photon flux density in the waveband 400 to 700 nm. For studies involving other wavebands, the waveband should be specified.

Use of Percentage in SI

Whenever the composition of some mixture is being described and it is possible to express elements of the mixture in SI base or derived units, the use of percent is unacceptable and should be replaced by appropriate SI units. For example, plant nutrient concentration must be expressed in SI units based on either amount of substance or mass.

When the elements of an event cannot be described in SI base or derived units, or when a well-known fractional comparison of an event is being described, percentage is acceptable. The following are examples where use of percentage is acceptable:

1. Coefficient of variation.
2. Botanical composition, plant stand, and cover estimates.
3. Percent leaves (or plants) infected.
4. Percent increase (or decrease) in yield.
5. Percent of applied element(s) that are recovered by plants, extractants, etc.
6. Fertilizer grades.
7. Percent relative humidity.
8. As an alternate unit of soil texture. This is allowed because each component is well defined and is a fraction on a mass basis.
9. As an alternate unit to express fractional base saturation. This is permissible because each component is a fraction on a chemical basis.
10. Atom percent abundance of a stable isotope, e.g., ^{15}N, ^{18}O. This is determined on a mass basis.

Parts per Thousand

The term parts per thousand, used in some mineralogy and oceanography references, is acceptable. This term is widely accepted for reporting isotope ratios relative to a standard and is dimensionless.

Parts per Million

Parts per million (ppm) is an ambiguous term. To avoid ambiguity, authors are required to use preferred or acceptable SI units as discussed. Depending on the type of data, authors could use $\mu L\ L^{-1}$, $mg\ L^{-1}$, or $mg\ kg^{-1}$ in place of parts per million. The only exception to the use of ppm is when associated with nuclear magnetic resonance (NMR) measurements. This is the official term used to express the relative shift of a NMR line of a given nucleus from the line associated with the standard for that nucleus. The term is dimensionless.

Cotton Fiber

Official standards for cotton staple length are given in terms of inches and fractions of an inch, generally in gradations of thirty-seconds of an inch. Stapling is done by a classer in comparison with staple standards. Measurement by instrument has shown unequal increments between consecutive staples in these standards. Because the classer is the authority on length, these unequal increments have been maintained. When staple length is determined by a classer, it may be reported as a code number with the code being the number of thirty-seconds of an inch called by the classer.

Instrument measurements are preferable in experimental work because of equal incremental differences between successive fiber lengths. These values should be reported using appropriate SI units (Table 6). Fiber fineness determined by the micronaire instrument should be reported as micronaire reading.

Recommended Units and Conversion Factors

Tables of recommended units (Table 6) and conversion factors (Table 7) are included to aid in the use of SI units.

Table 6. Examples of preferred (P) and acceptable (A) units for general use.

Quantity/Rate	Application	Unit	Symbol
Angle	X-ray diffraction pattern	radian (P)	θ
		degree (A)	°
Area	Land area	square meter (P)	m^2
		hectare (A)	ha
	Leaf area	square meter	m^2
	Specific surface area of soil	square meter per kilogram	$m^2\ kg^{-1}$
Interatomic spacing	Crystal structure	nanometer (P)	nm
		Angstrom (A)	Å
Bulk density (ρ_b)	Soil bulk density	megagram per cubic meter (P)	$Mg\ m^{-3}$
		gram per cubic centimeter (A)	$g\ cm^3$
Electrical conductivity†	Salt tolerance	siemen per meter	$S\ m^{-1}$
Elongation rate	Plant	milimeter per second (P)	$mm\ s^{-1}$
		millimeter per day (A)	$mm\ d^{-1}$
Ethylene production	N_2-fixing activity	nanomole per plant per second	$nmol\ plant^{-1}\ s^{-1}$
Extractable ion	Soil, mass basis	centimole per kilogram (P)	$cmol\ kg^{-1}$
		milligram per kilogram (A)	$mg\ kg^{-1}$
Extractable ion	Soil, volume basis	moles per cubic meter (P)	$mol\ m^{-3}$
		gram per cubic meter (P)	$g\ m^{-3}$
		centimole per liter (A)	$cmol\ L^{-1}$
		milligram per liter (A)	$mg\ L^{-1}$
Fertilizer rate	Soil	gram per square meter (P)	$g\ m^{-2}$
		kilogram per hectare (A)	$kg\ ha^{-1}$
Fiber strength	Cotton fiber	kilonewton meter per kilogram	$kN\ m\ kg^{-1}$
Flux density	Heat flow	watt per square meter	$W\ m^{-2}$
	Gas diffusion	mole per square meter per second (P)	$mol\ m^{-2}\ s^{-1}$
		gram per square meter per second (A)	$g\ m^{-2}\ s^{-1}$
	Water flow	kilogram per square meter per second (P)	$kg\ m^{-2}\ s^{-1}$
		cubic meter per square meter per second (A)	$m^3\ m^{-2}\ s^{-1}$
		meter per second (A)	$m\ s^{-1}$
Gas diffusivity	Gas diffusion	square meter per second	$m^2\ s^{-1}$
Grain test weight	Grain	kilogram per cubic meter	$kg\ m^{-3}$

(continued on next page)

Table 6. Continued.

Quantity/Rate	Application	Unit	Symbol
Growth rate	Plant growth	gram per square meter per day	g m^{-2} d^{-1}
Hydraulic conductivity	Water flow	kilogram second per cubic meter (P)	kg s m^{-3}
		cubic meter second per kilogram (A)	m^3 s kg^{-1}
		meter per second (A)	m s^{-1}
Ion transport	Ion uptake	mole per kilogram (of dry plant tissue) per second	mol kg^{-1} s^{-1}
		mole of charge per kilogram (of dry plant tissue) per second	mol$_c$ kg^{-1} s^{-1}
Leaf area ratio	Plant	square meter per kilogram	m^2 kg^{-1}
Length	Depth, width, and height	meter (P)	m
		centimeter (A)	cm
		millimeter (A)	mm
Magnetic flux density	Electronic spin resonance (ESR)	tesla	T
Nutrient concentration	Plant	millimole per kilogram (P)	mmol kg^{-1}
		gram per kilogram (A)	g kg^{-1}
Photosynthetic rate	CO$_2$ amount of substance flux density (P)	micromole per square meter per second (P)	μmol m^{-2} s^{-1}
	CO$_2$ mass flux density (A)	milligram per square meter per second (A)	mg m^{-2} s^{-1}
Precipitation	Rainfall	millimeter	mm
Resistance	Stomatal	second per meter	s m^{-1}
Soil texture composition	Soil	gram per kilogram (P)	g kg^{-1}
		percent (A)	%
Specific heat	Heat storage	joule per kilogram per kelvin	J kg^{-1} K^{-1}
Thermal conductivity	Heat flow	watt per meter per kelvin	W m^{-1} K^{-1}
Transpiration rate	H$_2$O flux density	gram per square meter per second (P)	g m^{-2} s^{-1}
		cubic meter per square per meter second (A)	m^3 m^{-2} s^{-1}
		meter per second (A)	m s^{-1}
Volume	Field or laboratory	cubic meter (P)	m^3
		liter (A)	L
Water content	Plant	gram water per kilogram wet or dry tissue (P)	g kg^{-1}
	Soil (acceptable for plants)	kilogram water per kilogram dry soil (P)	kg kg^{-1}
		cubic meter water per cubic meter soil (A)	m^3 m^{-3}
Wave number	IR spectroscopy	reciprocal centimeter	cm^{-1}
Yield	Grain or forage yield	gram per square meter (P)	g m^{-2}
		kilogram per hectare (A)	kg ha^{-1}
		megagram per hectare (A)	Mg ha^{-1}
		tonne per hectare (A)	t ha^{-1}
	Mass of plant or plant part	gram (gram per plant or plant part)	g (g plant^{-1} or g kernel^{-1})

† The term "electrolytic conductivity" has been substituted for "electrical conductivity" by the International Union of Pure and Applied Chemistry (IUPAC). Use of the SI term "electrolytic conductivity" is permissible but not mandatory in ASA publications at this time.

Table 7. Conversion factors for SI and non-SI units.

To convert Column 1 into Column 2, multiply by	Column 1 SI Unit	Column 2 non-SI Unit	To convert Column 2 into Column 1 multiply by
Length			
0.621	kilometer, km (10^3 m)	mile, mi	1.609
1.094	meter, m	yard, yd	0.914
3.28	meter, m	foot, ft	0.304
1.0	micrometer, μm (10^{-6} m)	micron, μ	1.0
3.94×10^{-2}	millimeter, mm (10^{-3} m)	inch, in	25.4
10	nanometer, nm (10^{-9} m)	Angstrom, Å	0.1
Area			
2.47	hectare, ha	acre	0.405
247	square kilometer, km² (10^3 m)²	acre	4.05×10^{-3}
0.386	square kilometer, km² (10^3 m)²	square mile, mi²	2.590
2.47×10^{-4}	square meter, m²	acre	4.05×10^3
10.76	square meter, m²	square foot, ft²	9.29×10^{-2}
1.55×10^{-3}	square millimeter, mm² (10^{-6} m)²	square inch, in²	645
Volume			
9.73×10^{-3}	cubic meter, m³	acre-inch	102.8
35.3	cubic meter, m³	cubic foot, ft³	2.83×10^{-2}
6.10×10^4	cubic meter, m³	cubic inch, in³	1.64×10^{-5}
2.84×10^{-2}	liter, L (10^{-3} m³)	bushel, bu	35.24
1.057	liter, L (10^{-3} m³)	quart (liquid), qt	0.946
3.53×10^{-2}	liter, L (10^{-3} m³)	cubic foot, ft³	28.3
0.265	liter, L (10^{-3} m³)	gallon	3.78
33.78	liter, L (10^{-3} m³)	ounce (fluid), oz	2.96×10^{-2}
2.11	liter, L (10^{-3} m³)	pint (fluid), pt	0.473

(continued on next page)

Table 7. Continued.

To convert Column 1 into Column 2, multiply by	Column 1 SI Unit	Column 2 non-SI Unit	To convert Column 2 into Column 1 multiply by
		Mass	
2.20×10^{-3}	gram, g (10^{-3} kg)	pound, lb	454
3.52×10^{-2}	gram, g (10^{-3} kg)	ounce (avdp), oz	28.4
2.205	kilogram, kg	pound, lb	0.454
0.01	kilogram, kg	quintal (metric), q	100
1.10×10^{-3}	kilogram, kg	ton (2000 lb), ton	907
1.102	megagram, Mg (tonne)	ton (U.S.), ton	0.907
1.102	tonne, t	ton (U.S.), ton	0.907
		Yield and Rate	
0.893	kilogram per hectare, kg ha^{-1}	pound per acre, lb acre^{-1}	1.12
7.77×10^{-2}	kilogram per cubic meter, kg m^{-3}	pound per bushel, lb bu^{-1}	12.87
1.49×10^{-2}	kilogram per hectare, kg ha^{-1}	bushel per acre, 60 lb	67.19
1.59×10^{-2}	kilogram per hectare, kg ha^{-1}	bushel per acre, 56 lb	62.71
1.86×10^{-2}	kilogram per hectare, kg ha^{-1}	bushel per acre, 48 lb	53.75
0.107	liter per hectare, L ha^{-1}	gallon per acre	9.35
893	tonnes per hectare, t ha^{-1}	pound per acre, lb acre^{-1}	1.12×10^{-3}
893	megagram per hectare, Mg ha^{-1}	pound per acre, lb acre^{-1}	1.12×10^{-3}
0.446	megagram per hectare, Mg ha^{-1}	ton (2000 lb) per acre, ton acre^{-1}	2.24
2.24	meter per second, m s^{-1}	mile per hour	0.447
		Specific Surface	
10	square meter per kilogram, m^2 kg^{-1}	square centimeter per gram, cm^2 g^{-1}	0.1
1 000	square meter per kilogram, m^2 kg^{-1}	square millimeter per gram, mm^2 g^{-1}	0.001

(continued on next page)

Table 7. Continued.

To convert Column 1 into Column 2, multiply by	Column 1 SI Unit	Column 2 non-SI Unit	To convert Column 2 into Column 1 multiply by
Pressure			
9.90	megapascal, MPa (10^6 Pa)	atmosphere	0.101
10	megapascal, MPa (10^6 Pa)	bar	0.1
1.00	megagram per cubic meter, Mg m^{-3}	gram per cubic centimeter, g cm^{-3}	1.00
2.09×10^{-2}	pascal, Pa	pound per square foot, lb ft^{-2}	47.9
1.45×10^{-4}	pascal, Pa	pound per square inch, lb in^{-2}	6.90×10^3
Temperature			
1.00 (K − 273)	Kelvin, K	Celsius, °C	1.00 (°C + 273)
(9/5 °C) + 32	Celsius, °C	Fahrenheit, °F	5/9 (°F −32)
Energy, Work, Quantity of Heat			
9.52×10^{-4}	joule, J	British thermal unit, Btu	1.05×10^3
0.239	joule, J	calorie, cal	4.19
10^7	joule, J	erg	10^{-7}
0.735	joule, J	foot-pound	1.36
2.387×10^{-5}	joule per square meter, J m^{-2}	calorie per square centimeter (langley)	4.19×10^4
10^5	newton, N	dyne	10^{-5}
1.43×10^{-3}	watt per square meter, W m^{-2}	calorie per square centimeter minute (irradiance), cal cm^{-2} min^{-1}	698
Transpiration and Photosynthesis			
3.60×10^{-2}	milligram per square meter second, mg m^{-2} s^{-1}	gram per square decimeter hour, g dm^{-2} h^{-1}	27.8
5.56×10^{-3}	milligram (H_2O) per square meter second, mg m^{-2} s^{-1}	micromole (H_2O) per square centimeter second, μmol cm^{-2} s^{-1}	180
10^{-4}	milligram per square meter second, mg m^{-2} s^{-1}	milligram per square centimeter second, mg cm^{-2} s^{-1}	10^4
35.97	milligram per square meter second, mg m^{-2} s^{-1}	milligram per square decimeter hour, mg dm^{-2} h^{-1}	2.78×10^{-2}

Plane Angle

	Column 1	Column 2	
57.3	radian, rad	degrees (angle), °	1.75×10^{-2}

Electrical Conductivity, Electricity, and Magnetism

	Column 1	Column 2	
10	siemen per meter, S m^{-1}	millimho per centimeter, mmho cm^{-1}	0.1
10^4	tesla, T	gauss, G	10^{-4}

Water Measurement

	Column 1	Column 2	
9.73×10^{-3}	cubic meter, m^3	acre-inches, acre-in	102.8
9.81×10^{-3}	cubic meter per hour, m^3 h^{-1}	cubic feet per second, ft^3 s^{-1}	101.9
4.40	cubic meter per hour, m^3 h^{-1}	U.S. gallons per minute, gal min^{-1}	0.227
8.11	hectare-meters, ha-m	acre-feet, acre-ft	0.123
97.28	hectare-meters, ha-m	acre-inches, acre-in	1.03×10^{-2}
8.1×10^{-2}	hectare-centimeters, ha-cm	acre-feet, acre-ft	12.33

Concentrations

	Column 1	Column 2	
1	centimole per kilogram, cmol kg^{-1} (ion exchange capacity)	milliequivalents per 100 grams, meq 100 g^{-1}	1
0.1	gram per kilogram, g kg^{-1}	percent, %	10
1	milligram per kilogram, mg kg^{-1}	parts per million, ppm	1

Radioactivity

	Column 1	Column 2	
2.7×10^{-11}	bequerel, Bq	curie, Ci	3.7×10^{10}
2.7×10^{-2}	bequerel per kilogram, Bq kg^{-1}	picocurie per gram, pCi g^{-1}	37
100	gray, Gy (absorbed dose)	rad, rd	0.01
100	sievert, Sv (equivalent dose)	rem (roentgen equivalent man)	0.01

Plant Nutrient Conversion

	Elemental	*Oxide*	
2.29	P	P$_2$O$_5$	0.437
1.20	K	K$_2$O	0.830
1.39	Ca	CaO	0.715
1.66	Mg	MgO	0.602

ABBREVIATIONS AND SYMBOLS

General

Using commonly accepted abbreviations and symbols saves space in the journals and saves time for the writer and reader. Excessive use of abbreviations, however, may confuse a reader with jargon and may give a choppy appearance to the printed page.

Rules for abbreviating and many accepted abbreviations are given in the *CBE Style Manual*. Note that few periods are used. Rules in other manuals may be helpful, but the periods used with many of the abbreviations given there are not acceptable in society publications. It is best to avoid using abbreviations in titles and abstracts. In the abstract, any abbreviations that seem necessary to use should be defined just as would be done in the main text.

Common Abbreviations

Accepted abbreviations and symbols are listed in the *CBE Style Manual* Additional useful points are as follows:

1. The SI units used with numerals are abbreviated. Do not use periods in abbreviating SI units of measurement.

2. The names of states, territories, and U.S. possessions should always be spelled in full when standing alone. When they follow the name of a city, use the two-letter U.S. Postal Service code form (Illinois, IL) with or without the zip code number.

3. The symbol % is used with arabic numbers. The symbol is not repeated with each number in a range or series. Do not use the word "percent" with a number.

4. Names of months accompanied by day and year are abbreviated, except May, June, and July. In text, the month should be spelled out when used alone, with only day or year, and at the beginning of sentences. The month should always be abbreviated in footnotes, tables, and references. See "Time and Dates," this chapter.

5. The initial(s) and last names of authors are used in the reference list and in footnotes. Full names may be used in by-lines.

6. The abbreviation or symbol of a unit of measurement should be used only if a number precedes the unit. The same abbreviation or symbol should be used for singular or plural forms of the unit.

7. At the beginning of a sentence, the unit of measurement that follows a spelled out number should also be spelled out. For example, "Fifteen liters is. . ." whereas, within a sentence use ". . .15 L is. . ."

8. Recognized symbols for chemical elements should be used without identification, e.g., N for nitrogen, except at the beginning of a sentence.

9. In a series of measurements, the unit(s) should be given at the end, i.e., 2 to 10 °C; 5, 10, and 20 kg ha^{-1}.

10. United States of America is abbreviated USA. United States also may be abbreviated USA. The abbreviation U.S. should be used only as a modifier, e.g., U.S. government, U.S. soybean crop. Well-known government units may be abbreviated, e.g., USDA-ARS, TVA, without spelling them out.

11. The Latin name of an organism should be spelled out the first time it is used in the abstract or in the paper. Thereafter, use only the first letter of the genus name and spell out the species name. If the Latin name begins a sentence, the genus name should be spelled out. Latin names are underlined (italicized).

12. The abbreviations "lat" and "long" should be used in expressions such as 30° N lat, 30° W long, 42°15'30" N lat. They are not needed when they are used together: 30° N, 20° W.

13. In a series of symbols or measurements where the first item begins a sentence, spell out only the first item, e.g., Nitrogen, P, K. . .

The following list of additional abbreviations is not exhaustive but gives the abbreviations commonly used in society publications. Use the same abbreviation for singular or plural items.

a.i.	active ingredient	EC	Enzyme Commission
Abstr.	Abstract	ed.	Editor(s) or Edition
Agric.	Agricultural or Agriculture	Eq.	equation (Eq. [2])
		Exp.	Experiment
Agron.	Agronomy	Fig.	figure (Fig. 6)
Am.	America or American	Gov.	Government
ARS	Agricultural Research Service	g (italic)	gravity, centrifugal
		h	hour
ASA	American Society of Agronomy	Handb.	Handbook
		i.d.	inside diameter
avg.	average	Illus.	Illustrations
CI	Cereal Investigation (CI 13880)	Inst.	Institute
		Int.	International
conc.	concentration	J.	Journal
Conf.	Conference	min	minute
Congr.	Congress	Monogr.	Monograph
Conserv.	Conservation	Natl.	National
Counc.	Council	no.	number
CSRS	Cooperative State Research Service	o.d.	outside diameter
		PI	plant introduction (PI 468960)
CSSA	Crop Science Society of America	Publ.	Publication, Publisher(s)
cv.	cultivar		
d	day	Rep.	Report
Dep.	Department	Res.	Research
diam.	diameter	s	second
dry wt.	dry weight	Sci.	Science

Serv.	Service	USDA	United States Department of Agriculture
Soc.	Society		
Spec.	Special	USEPA	United States Environmental Protection Agency
SSSA	Soil Science Society of America		
Stn.	Station	USSR	Union of Soviet Socialist Republics
TVA	Tennessee Valley Authority		
Univ.	University	Vol.	Volume
USA	United States of America	vs.	versus
		wk	week
		yr	year

SPELLING AND CAPITALIZATION

Webster's Third New International Dictionary of the English Language, Unabridged (Gove, 1964; or a later edition, if available) is the societies' primary guide to spelling, capitalization, and compounding. Use of another dictionary, such as *The Random House College Dictionary* (Urdang, 1972) is usually acceptable. The *CBE Style Manual* is a helpful reference, especially in specialized word spelling, and *The Chicago Manual of Style* covers the subject across a range of disciplines. Italics (underline in manuscript) are used for isolated foreign language wording likely to be unfamiliar to readers. Familiar words and scholarly abbreviations such as en masse, in vitro, in vivo, in situ, et al., e.g., i.e., or ca. are set in roman type and should not be underlined.

The following are common rules for capitalization (proper names, first word in sentence, etc.).

The first letter is capitalized for:

1. Regions, sections, or groups of sites commonly associated together, e.g., Corn Belt, North Central states, the South, the West, the Midwest; but northern Iowa.

2. First letter of genus, family, and order but not species.

3. Trademarked names. It is a misuse of a trademark to derive an adjective from it.

4. The first word after a colon if it begins a clause not logically dependent on the preceding clause.

5. Treatment 1, Day 2, Experiment 3, Year 4, etc.

6. Any title immediately preceding a name.

Do not capitalize titles when not preceding a name—e.g., assistant professor, research agronomist, and editor-in-chief—unless it is an official title, e.g., ASA Editor-in-Chief, but editor-in-chief of ASA.

Words derived from proper names but now in common usage are not capitalized; i.e., paris green, bunsen burner, petri dish. Do not capitalize names of grasses, e.g., bermudagrass, sudangrass; or seasons of the year, i.e., spring, summer, fall, winter.

NUMERALS

Reported data should include no more significant digits than the precision of the experimental methods warrant. Often, more than three significant digits of data from agronomic research cannot be justified. An acceptable rule is to round treatment means to one-tenth of their estimated standard error. For example, if the estimated standard error is 1.43, the means should be rounded to the nearest 0.1, and if the standard error is 18.4, the means should be rounded to the nearest 1.0.

Arabic numerals are generally preferable to roman numerals. Commas are not used to separate numbers greater than three digits. In text, four digit numbers are written together: 1000. A space separates numbers greater than four digits either left or right of the decimal point in tables and text: 10 000 and 0.052 067. In tables, when four-digit numbers and numbers of more than four digits occur together in a column, a space is used to separate the four-digit number: For example:

10

100

1 000

10 000

1 000 000

Dates, page numbers, percentages, time, numbers preceded by capitalized nouns, and numbers followed by units of measure are expressed as numerals: Table 1, Chapter 1, 2%, no. 1, Treatment 3, 1 g, 5 s, Eq. [1], etc. Words should be used otherwise to designate numbers below 10. A numeral is used for a single number of 10 or more, except when the number is the first word of the sentence. Numerals are used to designate the numbers nine and below when two or more numbers are used and any of them are above nine: ". . . 2, 5, and 20 pots were planted . . ." but ". . . a group of 12 plants was incubated at three temperatures." Ordinal numbers are treated like cardinal numbers: third, fourth, 33rd, 100th, except in references (e.g., 5th ed., 7th Congr.). Large numbers ending in zeros use a word for part of the number: 1.6 million (not 1 600 000) or 23 μg (not 0.000 023 g). A zero is used before decimal numbers less than 1.0: 0.1 and 0.5. Use the connecting word "to" rather than a dash in a range of numbers, except when the numbers are used in parentheses or in tables.

As discussed in the section on use of SI units, authors should avoid numbers with too many digits. Most often this is accomplished by selecting the proper prefix. Occasionally, particularly in the case of tables and figures, the unit will still have too many digits. Then units should be followed by a power of 10 by which the actual quantity was multiplied to produce the reported quantity. If authors are not careful in the choice of negative or positive exponents, readers will calculate a radically different number than the authors intended to present. The following examples illustrate the problem:

1. A reported entry of 6 under the heading m $\times$ 10^3 means that the actual value of m is 0.006.

2. A reported entry of 6 under the heading m $\times$ 10^{-3} means that the actual value of m is 6000.

3. A concentration of 0.0015 M can be expressed as either 1.5 under the heading "conc. (mM)," as 1500 under the heading "conc. (μM)," or as 15 under the heading "conc. (M) $\times$ 10^4."

PUNCTUATION

Punctuation marks help to show the meanings of words by grouping them into sentences, clauses, and phrases. These marks must be used precisely if the reader is to understand exactly the intended meaning.

The ordinary rules of punctuation are adequate for all ASA, CSSA, and SSSA publications. Some of these are given in the *CBE Style Manual* and *The Chicago Manual of Style*.

A few rules that are frequently violated are the following:

1. Use a comma before "and" or "or" in a series of three or more items, e.g., 2, 7, and 10 s.

2. Do not use a comma in a date that gives only the month and year, e.g., May 1965, or when one day of the month is given, e.g., 14 May 1965.

3. Do not use any punctuation after short items in a vertical list. For Example: 1. Stems
                          2. Roots
                          3. Leaves

4. If not otherwise identified as a cultivar, use single quotes around cultivar names the first time the names are introduced in the abstract or paper. Place punctuation outside of the single quote marks.

5. When it is necessary to enclose material within other statements already in parentheses, generally use brackets. For example: ". . .as stated (Jones, 1983 [as quoted by Smith, 1984])." Two exceptions to the use of brackets within parentheses are allowed for society publications. Use brackets if necessary to enclose scientific names that already contain parentheses, e.g., ". . .soybean [*Glycine max* (L.) Merr.] has the. . ." The use of brackets can usually be avoided by using commas. For example: ". . .soybean, *Glycine max* (L.) Merr., has the. . ." The other exception is mathematical usage, e.g., $A = [(b + c) - d] + e$. Also, numbered equations are referred to in text as Eq. [1] , Eq. [2], Eq. [3], etc.

6. Use the apostrophe when adding s for the plural only to avoid confusion, e.g., 1920s, ABCs, but M.A.'s.

COMPOUND WORDS AND DERIVATIVES (USE OF HYPHEN)

A work containing a prefix, suffix, or combining form is a derivative and is almost always written as one word. Compound words used to express an idea different from that expressed by the separate parts are usually written as one word. Hyphens are used to avoid a confusing sequence of letters, a confusing sequence of adjectives, a jumble of ideas, or possible confusion with a word of the same spelling without the hyphen, e.g., co-op, coop. Comprehensive rules for compounding are found in dictionaries and other books of usage.

Most compounds and derivatives fall under these general rules:

1. Derivatives are usually written solid, e.g., nonadditives, nonsignificant, postdoctoral, preemergent, antiquality, reuse, clockwise. Use hyphens with prefixes to words that begin with a capital and sometimes in a few awkward combinations that bring two vowels together, e.g., un-American, semi-independent. For correct spelling check *Websters Third New International Dictionary of the English Language, Unabridged.*

2. Hyphenate a compound adjective when used before, but not after, the word it modifies, e.g., winter-hardy plant; it is winter hardy; well-known method; it is well known.

3. Use a hyphen after a prefix to a unit modifier, e.g., semi-winter-hardy plant; non-winter-hardy plant.

4. Use a hyphen in a compound adjective that includes a number, including when the adjective is an abbreviated unit of measure, e.g., 10-yr-old field, 6-kg yield, 4-mm depth, 5- to 10-cm layer.

5. Noun compounds are usually formed when the term is a unit of measure or has special meaning or when one of the words has lost its accent, e.g., light-year, northeast, pineapple.

6. Do not use a hyphen after an adverb ending in -ly as the first part of a two-word modifier, e.g., widely known fact.

7. Use a hyphen for noun-adjective expressions for clarity; e.g., "On a per-gram basis."

8. Use hyphens to join numbers and abbreviations to chemical names, e.g., *trans*-2-bromocyclopentanol.

9. Use a short dash (–), rather than a hyphen, between components of a mixed chemical reagent when typing the manuscript, e.g., $HCl-H_2SO_4$.

TIMES AND DATES

Society publications use the 24-h time system, which is indicated by four digits—the first two for hours and the last two for minutes. In this system, the day begins at midnight, 0000 h, and the last minute is 2359 h. Thus, 2400 h of 31 Dec. 1987 is the same as 0000 h of 1 Jan. 1988. All time should be expressed with four digits, using a 0 where applicable, e.g., 0845 h.

The following style is used with the day of the month first, then the month, followed by the year: 18 Dec. 1987; 4 July 1987; but 18 December.

Julian day is frequently misused in biological literature to describe the calendar day of the year. The term is really the number of days from 1200 h on 1 Jan. 4713 B.C. A better term to describe the calendar day of the year is "day of the year."

MISCELLANEOUS STYLE POINTS

The usage advocated in this list is not exhaustive but merely covers some problem areas.

Abstract. Footnotes or literature references may not be used in the abstract.

Affect, Effect. These words are often confused by authors. Affect is usually correct as a verb. Never use it as a noun or as an adjective. Effect is always correct as a noun but can also be used as a verb. Correct: "light affects growth; light effects the conversion of chlorophyll to metastable products."

Commas. Use commas before changes of subject. Authors often use them when they are not needed. Try to break up nouns and clusters with commas when possible, e.g., "Dissolved in H_2O, NaCl forms a saline solution."

Cultivar Names. Use these names instead of repeating the genus and species or a long common name. Single quotes enclose the name the first time it is used unless the name is identified as being that of a cultivar. It is redundant to use the word cultivar and the abbreviation cv. or single quotes at the same time. Refer to *Registered Field Crop Varieties: 1926-1981* (CSSA, 1982) and other lists of published registrations for names of cultivars.

Foreign Numbers and Spellings. Use American spellings except for titles in references. Use sulfur not sulphur, unless in a citation.

Hardiness. Use Webster's: winterhardiness, winter-hardy plant, winter hardy.

However. Be careful of this word. It is most often used between commas as a transition word, but it may also be used as an adjective, e.g., ". . .however great the cost. . ." Use it rarely at the beginning of a sentence.

Nitrogen Fixation. Biological fixation of atmospheric nitrogen is correctly termed "dinitrogen fixation" and is represented in abbreviated form as "N_2 fixation" or "N_2-fixing ability."

None. Use a singular verb if none means *no one* or *not one* Use a plural verb only if the sense is *no two* or *no amount*. Examples: None of the books *was* on the shelf. None of the taxes *have* been paid. None of the scientists *agrees* on the same method.

Number. This word can be abbreviated to no. in tables, but it is best spelled out in text. There are exceptions: In methods and footnotes, it is permissible to use Plant no. 3 or a no. 3 needle. It is proper to use arabic number in this case and when scoring systems are used: "a scale of 0 to 5" rather than "a scale of zero to five."

Number of Sets of Chromosomes. Use $2x$, $3x$. The x's are not times signs and are set in italic.

Ranges. Use the connecting word "to" rather than a hyphen: -22.9 to $14.9\,°C$. Don't repeat $°C$. If the range is given in parentheses or in a table, use a short dash.

***Rhizobium*, Rhizobia, Rhizobial.** The word *Rhizobium* (italics) is a genus name that has only one meaning: it is the proper noun referring to the genus of bacteria. The collective noun "rhizobia" means more than one cell of *Rhizobium*. The adjective "rhizobial" describes some attributes of *Rhizobium*. Slow-growing rhizobia have been placed in a new genus, *Bradyrhizobium*.

Subscripts, Superscripts, Overbars, Accented Letters. Use these marks with discretion because they are difficult to typeset when several characters are used both as superscripts and subscripts.

Was, Were. Use "a total was," "data were," and "either was."

Which, That. "Which" introduces a nonrestrictive clause and is usually preceded by a comma (I do not drink sea water, which is salty.). "That" introduces a restrictive clause (I do not drink water that is salty.).

Chapter 6. Tables, Illustrations, and Mathematics

Tables and illustrations are used to support conclusions or illustrate concepts. Each figure or table should be entirely informative in itself. Text should be written around the tables and figures rather than appended to them. Tables and figures should be planned early in the writing of the manuscript and a minimum number of words used to describe them.

Tables and illustrations have essential differences in purpose. Tables present accurate numbers for comparison with other numbers. Illustrations reveal trends or record natural appearance. Sometimes these purposes overlap, but they rarely substitute for one another. Data presented in tables should not be duplicated in figures.

The rest of this chapter emphasizes technical preparation of tables, illustrations, and mathematical equations for society publications.

TABLES

Tables are used for reporting extensive numerical data in an organized manner. They should be self-explanatory. It is seldom necessary to use a table for fewer than eight items of data.

Table captions should be brief but sufficiently explain the data included. Captions *should not* include the units of measurement. Number the tables consecutively and refer to them in numerical order in the text as Table 1, Table 2, etc.

The principal parts of a table are shown on the following page. Follow this general form for the stub and field items. Show the units for all measurements: in spanner heads, in column heads, or in the field. In general, only horizontal rules are used: a single rule at the top, a single rule below the boxhead, and a single rule at the bottom just over the footnotes. Additional horizontal rules may be needed under spanner heads and subheads.

Table 1. Words and sentences.

Stub head§	Column head	Spanner head (if applicable to all columns)†		
		Subspanner head‡		
		Column head¶	Column head#	Column head††
unit	unit		unit	
(Stub)			(Field)	
		Independent line‡‡		
Main entry line				
Subentry line			536**	
Subsubentry line§§		208¶¶		
Subentry line				105*
		Independent line##		
Main entry line†††				
Subentry line				

*,**,*** Significant at the 0.05, 0.01, and 0.001 probability levels, respectively.
†, ‡, §, ¶, #, ††, …, ††† Supplementary notes.

Two types of footnotes are used with tables: those to show statistical significance and those to give supplementary information. The *, **, and *** are always used in this order to show statistical significance (or nonsignificance) at the 0.05, 0.01, and 0.001 probability levels, respectively, and cannot be used for other footnotes. Significance at other levels should be designated by a supplemental note. Lack of significance at any level is usually indicated by NS. Supplementary notes are given the following symbols in this order: †, ‡, §, ¶, #, ††, ‡‡, etc. These symbols should be cited just as you would read a table—from left to right and from top to bottom. Regardless of where asterisks appear in a table, they precede the other footnotes.

Draw footnote symbols by hand, if necessary, do not use numbers or letters. Indicate italics by underlining if italic lettering is not available on the typewriter used.

Numbers with the same unit and/or equal length should be centered in the column. If they are unequal, center the longest one and align the rest on the decimal point. If a column contains various units, like units should be aligned, but different units may be centered differently.

The use of exponentials is often necessary in tables. As explained in the section on numerals, care should be exercised when they are used. Unless the proper positive or negative exponent is used with the reported number, the reader will calculate a radically different number than the author meant to present.

The manuscript for tables should be typed double spaced. Type each table and its heading on a separate sheet. Additional information on tables is given in the *CBE Style Manual*.

FIGURES (ILLUSTRATIONS)

Figures are charts, graphs, or drawings; or photographs, photomicrographs, or other shaded material. Figures are often the best means of presenting scientific data. They are expensive to prepare and publish, however, so each should tell its "thousand words" or be omitted.

By far the most commonly used figures in technical journals are line or bar graphs, followed by line drawings, photomicrographs, and standard photographs. Photographs are more common in books, but graphs and charts still predominate in most books published by the three societies.

All figures should be of sufficient quality to allow adequate reproduction or they will be rejected by the managing editor.

The quality of all figures except photomicrographs is generally improved if they are published in a smaller size than they were originally drawn or photographed. With tri-society publications, the reproduction is typically at 40 to 60% of the original size, except for photomicrographs, which are published with little or no size reduction. This should be kept in mind, and figures prepared at about double the size they will appear in final published form. Figures should not be reduced to final size before they are sent to headquarters; the best quality is obtained when the reduction is done at the last step before printing.

The size of the published figure depends to some extent on where it will appear. For journals, a single column is approximately 85 mm (3.5 inches) wide, and full-page width is approximately 178 mm (7 inches). Books have a column width of approximately 114 mm (4.5 inches). Figures occasionally are placed lengthwise on a page (particularly in the case of photographs in books), but the practice is to be avoided when possible. Single-column, as opposed to two-column, figures are preferred in journals because they save both space and publication charges.

Captions

All captions must be typed double spaced, in numerical order, on a separate sheet, regardless of whether they also appear on the mounting paper with the figure itself.

A figure caption should be brief, but sufficiently explain the data so as to tell its own story. Identification of the curves or other parts, if possible, should be done in the figure itself and not in the caption. (This is more likely with charts and graphs than with photographs.) In both captions and text, refer to the figures with the abbreviation "Fig." Spell out the full word only when it appears as the first word of a sentence in the text.

Graphs and Charts (Line Drawings)

Graphs and charts improve the general presentation of a technical publication by reporting data in an easily comprehensible manner. They are used to show trends, not detailed information such as might be shown in a table.

The style of the drawings and the size and appearance of letters and numbers on the drawings should show continuity within a single paper and, ideally, from paper to paper within an issue. Seddigh and Jolliff (1988) have proposed a number of excellent suggestions in this regard. Many of those suggestions have been incorporated into the guidelines given here and all are worth considering. Copies of their paper are available at no charge from headquarters.

Drafting Materials

Use white drawing paper or tracing vellum and black india ink. Draw or mount the figure on 216- by 280-mm (8.5- by 11-inch) paper. Number each figure in the margin and include author(s) name(s) and, if needed, a short title on each one.

Size and Shape of Original Drawings

As already mentioned, drawings will be reduced 40 to 60% for best reproduction. This should be kept in mind not only in terms of the size of the drawing, but also in the size of the letters, numbers, and data points that appear on the drawing. More will be said about letters and numbers in a later section.

Seddigh and Jolliff (1988) suggest that whenever possible, figures be horizontal in format, with the height two-thirds the width. This format will not only take up a minimum amount of space in the journal (minimizing page charges), it will also facilitate reproduction as slides and for other purposes besides publication. The figures should be enclosed with a ruled line, not merely have X and Y axes at the bottom and left-hand side.

Thickness of Ruled Lines

The most important line in a graph is the derived curve; therefore it should be the darkest or heaviest line. Whenever possible, the curve should actually be a derived curve, not merely a series of straight lines connecting data points. If appropriate, the formula used to derive the curve should be included in the graph.

Next in importance are the individual data points; they should, therefore, be next in heaviness or darkness. Least important is the outline of the graph itself. Therefore, those lines should be the lightest ones of the figure.

If pens such as Leroy, Rapidograph, or Castell are used, a no. 2.5 or 3 point works well for the derived curves, a no. 2 for the data points, and a no. 1 for graph borders and interval marks.

Avoid using too many interval marks on the axes scales. It is not necessary to show all the coordinate ruling in most graphs. Satisfactory results will be obtained with only the necessary vertical and horizontal lines drawn in.

If various lines in the graph are identified by different markings or symbols, these should be identified within the graph rather than in the caption. Abbreviations should follow the same style used in the text.

Use the same symbols for data points for the same treatment throughout the manuscript. Symbols should also be large enough to withstand the reduction process. To achieve the desired minimum size of 1.5 mm in the finished version, they should be drawn approximately twice that size.

Photocopies of charts and graphs are sufficient for the review process, but the original art or a high-quality glossy photograph of it should be submitted for actual reproduction in the book or journal. If photographs of tables and charts are sent, they should measure at least 127 by 178 mm (5 by 7 inches).

PHOTOGRAPHS (SHADED MATERIAL)

Photographs should be taken under proper lighting conditions and with a suitable background that will not detract from the subject.

The reader should be provided with a reference point; one test plot can look much like another unless a specific focal point illustrates the significance of the message being conveyed. For example, a ruler can show plant height to describe the effects of various herbicides.

Position of the camera, cropping of the print or negative, and airbrushing can all be used to eliminate extraneous matter from the published version of the photograph. It is better to take a high-quality photograph in the first place, though, than to try to fix up a poor-quality one later.

If photos are taken in a series, the same height and angle of the camera, distance from the subject, and angle of the sun should be maintained. A picture taken 3 m from the subject at 0800 h will appear quite different from one taken of the same subject from 6 m at 1700 h.

Except for the occasional instance of full-color photos in certain books and monographs, only high-quality black-and-white glossy prints with sharp details and good contrast between light and dark areas should be used in publications. Prints should be in sharp focus and have good density. Color photos and illustrations made for slide projections or talks are rarely sharp enough or have sufficient contrast to reproduce well in journals or books.

In selecting photographs to be submitted for publication, authors should examine the photos to determine whether each shows something unique, interesting, and clearly identifiable. Photographs should be used only if they show something essential to the point being made.

It is good to have several photos of the same subject taken from different angles and under different lighting conditions. Authors then can select the one that shows the subject best. It is a good idea to save the other photos, in case the editor asks to see them. Negatives should be carefully saved. Prints will undergo a great deal of handling and the possibility of damage or loss always exists.

Carefully mark where the photo is to be cropped; 75 mm (3 inches) of empty sky above the subject is a costly use of journal or book space.

A suggested submission size for glossy prints is 200 by 250 mm (8 by 10 inches), but other sizes are acceptable. Small photomicrographs should be mounted.

Each of the four manuscript copies should include a full set of photographic prints of the original photos and photomicrographs. Photocopies are not acceptable substitutes for glossy prints.

When two or more photographs are to be combined into one figure, the parts should be mounted together on paper or light cardboard. Each part of the photograph(s) should be trimmed square and should lie flat and fit snugly together without paste or other mounting material visible around the margins. Each part of a composite figure should be clearly identified on the figure and/or in the caption by letters, e.g., A, B, C, etc. See the section on letters and numbers for details.

Although all figures must be identified, it is not good to write or type on the back of a photo, since the impression can show through on the front. Ideally, photos will be mounted, and the identification can be written on the paper or cardboard on which the photo is mounted. If there is no choice but to write on the back of a photo, write lightly with a soft lead pencil at the edge so as not to damage significant parts of the photo.

Ship photographs between sheets of cardboard to minimize possible damage in mailing and handling. Mounting each photograph separately on cardboard will provide additional protection from damage.

If a person or named product is shown in the photo, it is the responsibility of the author to obtain written permission for use of the photo from the person or the manufacturer of the product. The three societies are not responsible for any claims that may result.

LETTERS AND NUMBERS ON FIGURES

Size and Contrast

When letters or numbers (also arrows, scales, etc.) are needed on photographs, both size and contrast must be kept in mind. As previously mentioned, all photographs except photomicrographs will be published at 40 to 60% of their original size. Letters and numbers must be of sufficient original size to withstand this reduction. Recommended final size for letters and numbers on photos in journals and books is 1.5 to 1.75 mm (7- to 8-point type size). Letters and numbers on all photos except photomicrographs should, therefore, be twice this size in original form.

Letters, numbers, arrows, scales, etc. that appear in a light area of the photo should be black. If they appear in a dark area they should be white, or placed on a white circular or square background. Sufficient contrast is also essential for size bars used in photomicrographs.

A final size of 1.5 to 1.75 mm is also recommended for the smallest type on charts and graphs. Numbers and letters for main entries and headings should be somewhat larger; 2 to 2.75 mm (9- to 12-point type size). This means that the minimum size in original drawings for capital letters and numbers is 3.3 mm (14 points) and main entries and headings should be in the 4 to 5.5 mm range (18- to 24-point type size).

Style

To promote uniformity in lettering in the journal illustrations, authors and artists should use templates, lettering sets, dry transfer, or pressure-sensitive type on their graphs and charts. Freehand lettering and typewriter type are not acceptable.

Open style or block letters (usually referred to as sans serif) are the preferred style. If commercial pressure-sensitive or other forms of type are used, the recommended faces are Universe, Helvetica, or Helios, in 14-, 18-, and 24-point sizes. Chartpak is the trade name of one of the suppliers of this sort of type.

For mechanical lettering sets, Leroy template no. 140, 175, and 200; Rapidograph scriber series CL140, 175, and 200; and Rapidoguide no. 3031 and 3030 will give the desired style and height of lettering (between 3.5 and 5 mm). Use the no. 1 pen size with any of these.

Capital or Lowercase Letters

Use of all-capital letters is preferred for the primary axes labels, primary graph line labels, and other primary items in the illustration. Use lowercase letters for units of measure that follow the primary label.

For secondary headings within the illustration, use capital and lowercase letters (each main word starts with a capital letter) of the same letter (point) size as in the primary labels.

If additional subsidiary labels are needed in the illustration, use all capital letters in the next lower letter (point) size; i.e., 18-point letters for primary and secondary labels and 14-point capital letters for third-level labels. Do not make them less than 12 points (3 mm) in size.

The following figures show acceptable and unacceptable examples.

Mechanical Lettering Guides

RECOMMENDED TEMPLATE & PEN COMBINATIONS IN ACTUAL SIZE

The chart shows the wide range of LEROY lettering effects that can be produced by combining various LEROY templates and pens.

*These template and pen sizes should be your first choice.

Capital letter height, mm	Template size	Pen size			
		0	1	2	3
2.0	80	C			
2.5	100	B	C	D	
3.1	120	C	D	E	
3.6	140*	C	D*	E	F
4.5	175*	C	D*	E	F
5.1	200*	C	D*	E	F
6.1	240	C	D	E	F

Dry Transfer of Pressure-Sensitive Letters

UNIVERS 55   *All lettering shown actual size*

14 POINT —
ABCDEFGHIJKLMNOPQRSTUVWX
abcdefghijklmnopqrstuvwx   1234567890

18 POINT —
ABCDEFGHIJKLMNOPQR
abcdefghijklmnopqr   1234567890

24 POINT —
ABCDEFGHIJKLM
abcdefghijklm   12345678

UNACCEPTABLE

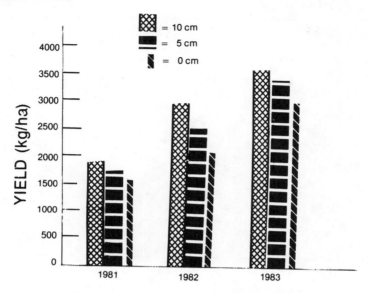

This figure is unacceptable for a number of reasons. The patterns used on the bars are complicated and confusing, the bars themselves are of varying widths. Also the numbers are too small for good reproduction in journal size.

ACCEPTABLE

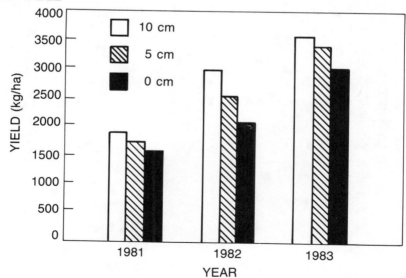

Larger typefaces, clear and simple patterns, and adequately sized type make for a figure that is much easier to understand. Also the figure is boxed in and in the recommended horizontal, rather than vertical format.

UNACCEPTABLE

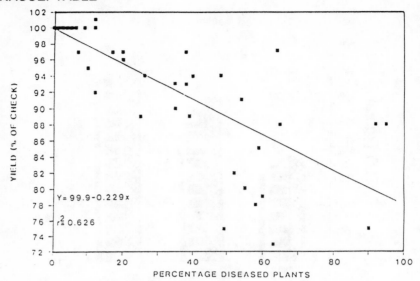

The line weights are opposite of what is recommended and some of them, and the type, are
too light for good reproduction.

ACCEPTABLE

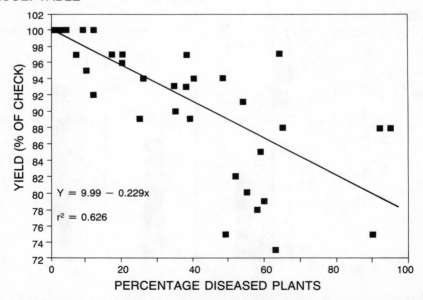

The line weights in this figure are as recommended; the derived curve the darkest, data points
next darkest, and the figure outline the lightest. Even the lightest, though, are dark enough
for adequate reproduction.

IMPORTANT SUGGESTIONS FOR FIGURES

1. Never use typewriter or hand-drawn letters for illustrations.

2. Be sure that the decimal points are correctly positioned and large enough to stand reduction in size. The size of the decimal point should be in proportion to the accompanying numbers. Place the decimal points at the base of the numbers, not centered halfway up as is done in some European journals.

3. Use sharp glossy photographs for drawings if the originals are filed or very large. Be sure the photographs are 200 by 250 mm (8 by 10 inches) and that no distortion or out- of-focus areas have been allowed in the printing process.

4. Clearly label all illustrations along the top or bottom margin indicating the author and the figure number. Also, indicate which edge is the top of the illustration.

5. Computer-generated graphs are acceptable for society publications *only* if they meet the standards discussed above; many are not acceptable. Most problems in reproduction lie in uneven type and broken lines. Make all lines, letters, and numbers using continuous solid black lines. Consult your computer programmer for proper combinations of type size and density of characters on the printout.

6. Use the same abbreviations for units of measurement in the figures as were used in the text.

7. Do not send photographs or drawings that require enlarging. If this is necessary, have the enlargement made locally and check it for quality before deciding on its use.

8. Make lines straight and corners square.

9. Use solid black, white, diagonal lines, dot screen, or a random dot for bar graph patterns. Do not use decorative borders.

MATHEMATICAL EQUATIONS

Mathematical equations give journals and books some of their most difficult and costly problems of type composition. If equations are not clearly and unmistakably marked in the manuscript, they may cause errors in any step along the way from the copy editor to the compositor, proofreader, author, and back to the editor. What may be perfectly clear to the author can be bewildering to anyone who is not a mathematician. Keep in mind that typesetters will reproduce what they see, and not what you know. Therefore, preparation of the manuscript copy and all directions and identification of letters and symbols must be clear, so that those lacking in mathematical expertise can follow the copy.

Position and Spacing

Positions, spacings, and other details must be exactly as they are to appear in printed form. If your typewriter does not have special symbols, draw them in neatly by hand. Draw or type superscript and subscript letters and symbols in the correct positions, and mark them in pencil if there might be any confusion about them, e.g., e^x, $\log_{10}$, B_{c_2}. The typist must put the proper space before and after mathematical symbols. For example, use a hyphen with spaces on both sides for the minus sign, but omit the space after the hyphen when the sign represents a negative quantity, e.g., $5 - 2 = 3$; a range from -15 to $+25$ kg.

Identifying Characters

Call attention in pencil marks to obscure modifications of symbols, e.g., prime marks, dots over symbols, and similar notation. Carefully distinguish between the letter "O" and zero; the letter "I," lowercase L, and the number "1"; and the degree symbol and the superior letter "o" or zero. When "x" represents the multiplication sign, indicate this lightly in pencil marks or write "multi. sign" above it. Indicate desired type size and face as follows: capitals—triple underline, small capitals—double underline, italic type—single underline, and boldface type—wavy underline. Identify these characters in text as well as in equations and tables. Single letters that denote mathematical constants, variables, and unknown quantities in text and in equations should be in italic. Vectors are set in boldface roman type.

Fractions and Simplifying Equations

Use slant rule fractions (e.g., x/y) as much as possible, especially in the text. Show the necessary aggregation by using parentheses, brackets, and braces. Use the sequence $\{[( )]\}$.

In horizontal rule fractions, be sure to align the rules with the main signs of the equation or formula. In complex equations, use horizontal rules for the main fractions and slant rules in numerators, denominators, and exponents.

Use	Instead of
a/bcd	$\dfrac{a}{bcd}$
$a/(b - c)$	$\dfrac{a}{b - c}$
$(a/c) - (b/d)$	$\dfrac{a}{c} - \dfrac{b}{d}$

Exponential Functions

For exponentials with lengthy or complicated exponents, the symbol exp should be used, particularly if such exponentials appear in the body of the text. Thus, $\exp (a^2 + b^2)^{1/2}$ is preferable to $e^{(a^2 + b^2)^{1/2}}$. The larger size of symbols permitted by this usage also makes reading easier. In index size the structure of some of the complicated exponents may entail expensive hand setting.

Integral Signs and Limits

With single integral signs, the upper and lower limits should always be placed to the right of the integral sign, never above and below.

$$\int_z^a \quad \text{not} \quad \int\limits_z^a$$

Radical Signs

Use fractional and negative exponents, wherever possible, instead of the radical sign and fractions. The following example illustrates conversion with the fractional exponent and also the saving in space which may be made with the use of the solidus or slant line. should be written

$$\frac{\cos \frac{1}{x}}{\sqrt{a + \frac{b}{x}}} \quad \text{should be written} \quad \frac{\cos (1/x)}{[a + (b/x)]^{1/2}}$$

If the radical sign is necessary, use the partial rather than the complete sign, e.g., $\sqrt{(x/y)}$ instead of $\sqrt{(x/y)}$.

Accented Letters and Symbols

Some accented letters are a typesetting problem, such as accents on Greek letters or lowercase letters with ascenders (e.g., σ, b). Avoid extensive use of symbols or letters with accents or bars placed directly above or below. Try to use primes, suffixes, or asterisks, e.g., use a' or $a*$ instead of a, a, or a. To designate "average," use pointed brackets instead of an overbar; $<a + b>$, not $\overline{a + b}$.

Numbering Equations

It is not necessary to number all displayed equations. Usually only those that are referred to elsewhere are numbered. If equations are numbered, place the numbers in brackets at the right margin. Refer to them in the text as Eq. [1], Eq. [10], etc.

Additional References for Mathematics

More information on rules and suggestions in preparing mathematical copy can be found in the *CBE Style Manual* and in other references listed in the bibliography.

Greek Letters

Unless special typewriter keys are available, a fine-point pen or pencil should be used for making Greek letters. These letters should be identified in the margins the first time they appear and should be marked whether capital or lowercase, e.g., "cap. beta" or "l.c. sigma."

The Greek alphabet, showing both capital and lowercase letters, is given below. Modifications of a few of these letters may be acceptable, but the ones given here should be used insofar as possible.

	Capital	Lower case		Capital	Lower case		Capital	Lower case
alpha	A	α	iota	I	ι	rho	P	ρ
beta	B	β	kappa	K	κ	sigma	Σ	σ, ς
gamma	Γ	γ	lambda	Λ	λ	tau	T	τ
delta	Δ	$\delta\ \partial$	mu	M	μ	upsilon	Υ	υ
epsilon	E	ϵ	nu	N	ν	phi	Φ	ϕ, φ
zeta	Z	ζ	xi	Ξ	ξ	chi	X	χ
eta	H	η	omicron	O	o	psi	Ψ	ψ
theta	Θ	θ, ϑ	pi	Π	π	omega	Ω	ω

Chapter 7. Proofreading

Galley, figure, table, or page proofs, along with manuscripts for all articles, are sent to authors for review before the articles are published. The authors are responsible for the careful proofing and prompt return of the proofs and manuscripts. Authors should answer all questions from the editors. Such questions may be found in memos or marked in the margins of the proofs or manuscript.

The editors, typesetters, and printers exercise great care in avoiding and correcting errors, but they cannot assume responsibility for any that are not marked by the author on the proofs. The author is entirely responsible for the correct spelling of names and for other information given in citations and for citing the references in the proper places in the text. Authors are also responsible for the accuracy of all facts, dates, statistics, and the position of all parts of mathematical formula.

Keep in mind that the proof is handled differently than the manuscript. Corrections in the manuscript copy are made within the line at the point of correction. The compositor reads along line by line and sets the type from the corrected manuscript. But once the type has been set and the copy is in proof form, the editor and compositor will no longer read each line to find where changes have to be made. Instead, they will look down the margins of the proofs to find the appropriate proofreader's mark opposite the line where a correction is needed. Therefore, mark all corrections in the margin of the proof.

Read the proof twice—first with another person reading aloud from the manuscript. This will help to avoid omissions of full lines or paragraphs, errors in dates, statistics, and mathematical formula. Check all references to tables, figures, and literature citations. Read the proof a second time alone. Be careful that your eyes do not pass over misspellings and omissions.

A sample corrected proof and some common proofreader's marks are shown on the next pages. Study the sample proof and the proofreader's marks carefully before checking actual proofs. Actual proofs will need only a fraction of the corrections shown in the sample. Authors should not let the seeming lack of errors lull them into complacency so that they miss the few errors that are most likely there. Keep the following points in mind (see also *CBE Style Manual*, p. 105-111):

1. Use red ink or red pencil for correction marks; write legibly. Place all correction marks in the margins of the proofs, either left or right, opposite the line in which the error occurs. If there are a large number of corrections in one line or in an adjoining line, use both left and right margins for marking.

2. Make two marks on the proof for each correction: one or more in the text line using a caret and short perpendicular line ($\land$) to show *where* the change is needed, and the other in the margin to show *what* change is needed.

3. Cross out unwanted characters and put a delete sign in the margin when material is to be deleted. When material is to be substituted for a deletion, don't use the delete sign; just cross out the unwanted material and write the new copy in the margin.

4. If there are several corrections in one line, separate one from another by slant lines (e.g., $\land$ /$\ominus$/$\oslash$) and arrange them in order to read from left to right. If the same correction is made in two or more places in the same line or in adjoining lines, write the correction once and follow it with a number of slant lines to equal the number of corrections.

5. Type insertions of more than one line at the bottom of the proof or type them on a separate sheet and attach the sheet to the proof with tape. Show clearly where new copy is to be inerted. All changes must be on the galley proof and not in a separate letter or note.

6. If a word, phrase, or sentence is substituted in a paragraph, make the substitution as nearly as possible the same number of letters as the deleted matter. If possible, delete at the end of a paragraph rather than in the middle or at the beginning.

7. Transposing words, phrases, or sentences is costly. Transposing paragraphs is relatively inexpensive.

8. Always make changes or answer questions on the proof, *never* on the manuscript.

9. Look for question marks on the manuscript and proofs. Give a clear answer to every query from the editor or typesetter.

10. Only essential changes should be requested. Authors of journal articles will be charged for revisions or additions to the proofs that are changes from the original manuscript. Author errors or additions should be indicated on the proof with a circled "AA."

11. Printer's errors (deviations from the original copy) are corrected at no cost to the author. Any printer's errors detected should be indicated on the proof with a circled "PE."

12. Indicate the position of figures and tables by a marginal notation with a circle around it; also encircle all notes, etc., not to be set in type.

13. Proofs of tables and figures at their final sizes are included with the text proofs. The table proofs should be carefully proofread; mark corrections directly on the proof. Check the figures to be sure they are accurate and correctly identified.

14. The desired return date for the proofs is indicated. Use airmail for locations outside the USA and first-class mail within the USA.

When proofs are returned, the production editor looks them over carefully, edits the changes or additions if necessary, and transfer the corrections to another set of proofs. The corrections are made to the typeset material prior to final page make up.

SAMPLE PROOF

Mean symptom readings (Table 1 showed that)

Avena sterilis lines were more resistant than the *A.*

sativa checks and that the resistance was transmitted

to F/1 and F_2 hybrids with Lamar. The dominance ef-

fects were consistently smaller than the cumlative addi-

tive effects and did not differ signifi cantly from zero in

six cases out of eight (Table 1). although these results

indicate that inheritance of resistance was determined

predominantly by additive gene action, they should not

be taken as proof that dominance was not involved. In

fact, the performmances of the F_1's (Table 1, Fig 1)

were not at the midpoint between those of their parents

but were closer to those of the resistant A. sterilis

parental lines, suggesting some dominance for resistance.

PROOFREADER'S MARKS

∧ Caret—something to be inserted; mark in text line

⊙ Period

∧ Comma

⊙ ∧ /: Colon

;/ Semicolon

∨ Apostrophe

∨/∨ Quotations

=/ n /н Hyphen

(/) Parentheses

⌊ / ⌋ Brackets

☐ Indent one em, double for two em, and so on

1/M One em dash (long dash)

1/N One en dash (short dash)

1/H Hyphen

◡ Close up

stet Let it stand, when something has been inadvertently crossed out. Dots under matter will usually suffice, but also include "stet" on margin to avoid misunderstanding.

✶, ⤴ Delete—take out

⤴ Delete and close up

X Broken letters or defective type

¶ Paragraph

no ¶ No paragraph

wf Wrong font

≡ Capitals and *caps*

⹀ Small capitals and *sc*

less ⓐ Less space

ⓘ Insert space

eq ⓢ Equalize spacing

⊙ Turn letter or line

[*or*] Move to left or to right

⊓ *or* ⊔ Move up or move down

tr Transpose

(b a) Character to go around letters, words, or phrases to *tr* indicate that they are to be transposed. Always include "tr" on margin of proof.

lc Lower case

\2/ Superior letter or figure

/a\ Inferior letter or figure

——— Italics and *ital*

rom Roman

bf Boldface

⑦ Circle around figures means spell out

(twenty) (grams) Circle around word means use figure or abbreviation.

Correction requires two marks on the proof—one in the margin indicating what is to be done and another within the type indicating by a short perpendicular line or a caret (/) the exact place where the change is to be made.

Chapter 8. Copyright and Permission to Print

To comply with the provisions of the U.S. Copyright Law of 1978 (P.L. 94-553), the three societies handle copyright and permissions in the following ways.

1. A Permission to Print and Reprint Form is used when the societies do not intend to copyright an individual article in a publication. Authors of such articles, when signing the form, retain the authority and responsibility to decide upon and respond to requests for further use by other persons or organizations.

2. A Transfer of Copyright Form is used for publications where the individual articles are copyrighted by the societies. Details of the transfer agreement are given on the form.

Each of these forms has two check items, one for authors who are U.S. government employees and the other for nongovernment authors. Generally, work done by government employees on government time is in the public domain and cannot be copyrighted; but the form certifies how the work was done.

The copyright law also requires that permission be obtained to use copyrighted material that was published elsewhere. It is the author's responsibility to obtain permission from the owner of material not in the public domain. A letter should be sent requesting permission. The signed letter granting permission should be attached to the manuscript so that it can be permanently filed at ASA Headquarters.

Name and address of
copyright owner

Dear

    I am writing an article entitled _____
_____
_____
to be published in _____ .
    I request your permission to include in my article the following material:
_____
_____
_____
Volume _____ Page(s) _____ Year _____ from the article
_____
written by _____ .
    If you grant your permission, please sign in the space below and return
this letter to me. Thank you.

                               Sincerely,

Permission to use the above-cited material in the publication described above,
and the subsequent reprints, editions, and translations of it in a nonexclusive
manner is granted, provided proper credit to the author and publisher is made.

By _____   _____
               Print name   Sign name

Date _____   Title _____

Sample letter for requesting permission to reproduce material from another source.

Chapter 9. Publication Title Abbreviations

Adv. Agron.	Advances in Agronomy
Agric. Eng.	Agricultural Engineering
Agronomy	Agronomy (Monographs)
Agron. J.	Agronomy Journal
Am. J. Bot.	American Journal of Botany
Am. Mineral.	American Mineralogist
Am. Soc. Test. Mater.	American Society for Testing and Materials
Anal. Chem.	Analytical Chemistry
Ann. App. Biol.	Annals of Applied Biology
Ann. Bot. (city of location)	Annals of Botany (London), Annals of Botanici (Fennici), etc.
Annu. Rev. Microbiol.	Annual Review of Microbiology
Aust. J. Agric. Res.	Australian Journal of Agricultural Research
Aust. J. Plant Physiol.	Australian Journal of Plant Physiology
Biochem. J.	Biochemical Journal
Bot. Gaz. (Chicago)	Botanical Gazette
Can. J. Genet. Cytol.	Canadian Journal of Genetics and Cytology
Can. J. Plant Sci.	Canadian Journal of Plant Science
Can. J. Soil Sci.	Canadian Journal of Soil Science
Clay Miner. Bull.	Clay Minerals Bulletin
Clays Clay Miner.	Clays and Clay Minerals
Crop Sci.	Crop Science
Crops Soils	Crops and Soils Magazine
Discuss. Faraday Soc.	Discussions of the Faraday Society
Environ. Sci. Technol.	Environmental Science and Technology
Ind. Eng. Chem.	Industrial and Engineering Chemistry
J. Agric. Food Chem.	Journal of Agricultural and Food Chemistry
J. Agron. Educ.	Journal of Agronomic Education
J. Am. Soc. Sugar Beet Technol.	Journal of the American Society of Sugar Beet Technologists
J. Atmos. Sci.	Journal of Atmospheric Sciences
J. Appl. Bacteriol.	Journal of Applied Bacteriology
J. Appl. Phys.	Journal of Applied Physics
J. Assoc. Off. Anal. Chem.	Journal of the Association of Official Analytical Chemists
J. Biol. Chem.	Journal of Biological Chemistry
J. Br. Grassl. Soc.	Journal of the British Grassland Society

J. Colloid Sci.	Journal of Colloid Science
J. Econ. Entomol.	Journal of Economic Entomology
J. Environ. Qual.	Journal of Environmental Quality
J. Fert. Issues	Journal of Fertilizer Issues
J. Hered.	Journal of Heredity
J. Meteorol.	Journal of Meteorology
J. Prod. Agric.	Journal of Production Agriculture
J. Sediment. Petrol.	Journal of Sedimentary Petrology
J. Soil Water Conserv.	Journal of Soil and Water Conservation
J. Water Pollut. Control Fed.	Journal of the Water Pollution Control Federation
Mineral. Mag.	Mineralogical Magazine
NACTA J.	National Assocation of Colleges and Teachers of Agriculture Journal
Natl. Bur. Stand.	National Bureau of Standards
Nature (City of location)	Nature (London), Nature (Moscow), etc.
N.Z. J. Agric. Res.	New Zealand Journal of Agricultural Research
Nucl. Sci. Abstr.	Nuclear Science Abstracts
Phytopathology	Phytopathology
Plant Physiol.	Plant Physiology
Plant Soil	Plant and Soil
Proc. Am. Soc. Hortic. Sci.	Proceedings of the American Society for Horticultural Science
Proc. Int. Grassl. Congr., 7th, 1956	1960 Proceedings of the International Grassland 7th Congress
Proc. Int. Seed Test. Assoc.	Proceedings of the International Seed Testing Association
Proc. Natl. Acad. Sci. USA	Proceedings of the National Academy of Sciences of the United States of America
Proc. Soil Crop Sci. Soc. Fla.	Proceedings of the Soil and Crop Science Society of Florida
Residue Rev.	Residue Reviews
Science (City of location)	Science (Washington, DC), Science (Tokyo), etc.
Soil Sci.	Soil Science
Soil Sci. Soc. Am. Proc.	Soil Science Society of America Proceedings
Soil Sci. Soc. Am. J.	Soil Science Society of America Journal
Soil Surv. Horiz.	Soil Survey Horizons
Soils Fert.	Soils and Fertilizers
Trans. Am. Geophys. Union	Transactions of the American Geophysical Union
Trans. Int. Congr. Soil Sci., 9th, 1968	Transactions of the 9th International Congress of Soil Science
Trans. Jt. Meet. Comm. 4, 5, Int. Soc. Soil Sci., 1962	Transactions of Joint Meeting of Commissions IV & V, International Society of Soil Science
Water Resour. Res.	Water Resources Research

References

Brickell, D.D. (ed.). 1980. International code of nomenclature of cultivated plants. Regnum Veg. 104.

Carmer, S.G., and W.M. Walker. 1982. Baby bear's dilemma: A statistical tale. Agron. J. 74:122–124.

Chemical Abstracts Service. 1984. Chemical Abstracts Service source index: 1907–1984 cumulative, plus annual supplements. Chem. Abstr. Serv., Columbus, OH.

Chew, V. 1976. Comparing treatment means: A compendium. HortScience 11:348–357.

Council of Biology Editors. 1983. CBE style manual. 5th ed. Counc. of Biol. Ed., Bethesda, MD.

Crop Science Society of America. 1982. Registered field crop varieties: 1926–1981. CSSA, Madison, WI.

Crop Science Society of America, Terminology Committee. 1988. Glossary of crop science terms. CSSA, Madison, WI.

Dodd, J.S. (ed.). 1986. The ACS style guide: A manual for authors and editors. Am. Chem. Soc., Washington, DC.

Dybing, C.D. 1977. Letter from the editor (on light intensity). Crop Sci. 17:ii (March–April).

French, C.W., E.A. Powell, and H. Angione (ed.). 1980. The Associated Press stylebook and libel manual. Addison-Wesley Publ. Co., New York.

Gove, P.B. (ed.). 1964. Webster's third new international dictionary of the English language, unabridged. G. and C. Merriam Co., Springfield, MA.

Guthrie, R.L., and J.E. Witty. 1982. New designations for soil horizons and layers and the new soil survey manual. Soil Sci. Soc. Am. J. 46:443–444.

Leonard, W.H., R.M. Love, and M.E. Heath. 1968. Crop terminology today. Crop Sci. 8:257–261.

Little, T.M. 1978. If Galileo published in HortScience. HortScience 13:504–506.

Meister Publishing Co. (Updated yearly). Farm chemicals handbook. Meister Publ. Co., Willoughby, OH.

Nelson, L.A., and J.O. Rawlings. 1983. Ten common misuses of statistics in agronomic research and reporting. J. Agron. Educ. 12:100–105.

Petersen, R.G. 1977. Use and misuse of multiple comparison procedures. Agron. J. 69:205–208.

Seddigh, M., and G.D. Jolliff. 1988. Recommendations on preparation of line graphs for presentation of scientific data. J. Agron. Educ. 17:3–6.

Shibles, R. 1976. Committee report. Terminology pertaining to photosynthesis. Crop Sci. 16:437–439.

Soil Management Support Services. 1985. Keys to soil taxonomy. Technical monograph 6, second printing. Dep. of Agronomy, Cornell Univ., Ithaca, NY.

Soil Science Society of America, Terminology Committee. 1987. Glossary of soil science terms. SSSA, Madison, WI.

Soil Survey Staff. 1975. Soil taxonomy: A basic system of soil classification for making and interpreting soil surveys. USDA-SCS Agric. Handb. 436. U.S. Gov. Print. Office, Washington, DC.

University of Chicago Press. 1982. The Chicago manual of style. 13th ed. Univ. of Chicago Press, Chicago.

Urdang, L. (ed.). 1972. The Random House college dictionary. Random House, New York.

U.S. Department of Agriculture. 1982–1986. National soil taxonomy handbook, Issues 1–9. USDA-SCS, Washington, DC.

U.S. Government Printing Office. 1984. Style manual. U.S. Gov. Print. Office, Washington, DC.

Other Useful Literature

American Chemical Society, Biological Abstracts and Engineering Index. 1974. Bibliographic guide for editors and authors. Chem. Abstr. Serv., Columbus, OH.

American Institute of Physics. 1978. Style manual. 3rd ed., rev. D. Hathwell and A.W.K. Metzner (ed.) Am. Inst. of Physics, New York.

American Mathematical Society. 1973. A manual for authors of mathematical papers. Am. Math. Soc., Providence, RI.

American Society of Agricultural Engineers, Cultural Practices Equipment Committee. 1986. Terminology and definitions for agricultural tillage implements. p. 310–319. *In* R.H. Hahn and E.E. Rosentreter (ed.) ASAE standards 1986. ASAE, St. Joseph, MI.

American Society for Testing and Materials. 1980. ASTM standard for metric practice E380-79. ASTM, Philadelphia, PA.

Bates, R.L., and J.A. Jackson (ed.). 1980. Glossary of geology. 2nd ed. Am. Geological Inst., Alexandria, VA.

Campbell, G.S., and J. van Schilfgaarde. 1981. Use of SI units in soil physics. J. Agron. Educ. 10:73–74.

DeBakey, L. 1976. The scientific journal: Editorial policies and practices. C.V. Mosby Co., St. Louis, MO.

Entomological Society of America. 1982. Common names of insects and related organisms. Entomol. Soc. of Am., College Park, MD.

Incoll, L.D., S.P. Long, and M.R. Ashmore. 1977. SI units in publications in plant science. Curr. Adv. Plant Sci. 28:331–342.

Little, T.M., and F.J. Hills. 1980. Statistical methods in agricultural research. John Wiley & Sons, New York.

National Bureau of Standards. 1977. International system of units. Spec. Publ. 30. U.S. Gov. Print. Office, Washington, DC.

O'Connor, M. 1979. The scientist as editor. John Wiley & Sons, New York.

Skillin, M.E., R.M. Gay, and other authorities [sic]. 1974. Words into type. 3rd ed. Prentice-Hall, Englewood Cliffs, NJ.

Snedecor, G.W., and W.G. Cochran. 1967. Statistical methods. 6th ed. Iowa State Univ. Press, Ames, IA.

Steel, R.G.D., and J.H. Torrie. 1980. Principles and procedures of statistics. 2nd ed. McGraw-Hill Book Co., New York.

Strunk, W., Jr., and E.B. White. 1959. The elements of style. Macmillan Co., New York.

Terrell, E.E. (No date). Guidelines for using scientific names of plants in manuscripts. ARC, USDA Publ. PSR-26-72.

Terrell, E.E., S.R. Hill, J.H. Wiersma, and W.E. Rice. 1986. A checklist of names for 3000 vascular plants of economic importance. USDA-ARS Agric. Handb. 505. U.S. Gov. Print. Office, Washington, DC.

Thien, S.J., and J.D. Oster. 1981. The international system of units and its particular application to soil chemistry. J. Agron. Educ. 10:62–70.

Vorst, J.J., L.E. Schweitzer, and V.L. Lechtenberg. 1981. International system of units (SI): Application to crop science. J. Agron. Educ. 10:70–72.

Weed Science Society of America. 1971. Composite list of weeds. Weed Sci. 20:435–476.

West, T.S. 1978. Recommendations on the usage of the terms "equivalent" and "normal." Pure Appl. Chem. 50:325–338.

Woodford, F.P. (ed.). 1968. Scientific writing for graduate students. Rockefeller Univ. Press, New York.

Index